Indigos

Indigos

© 2011 Aquila Media Productions
PO Box 2884
Addison, TX 75001
www.aquilamediaproductions.com

Portions of this book were originally published under the title
Understanding Your Life through Awareness by Kathy Altaras.

Cover design, layout, and graphic additions: Dallas Drotz, Drotz Design

Library of Congress Cataloging-in-Publication Data

Altaras, Kathy
      Indigos: The Quiet Storm

ISBN 978-0-9822705-2-3

LCCN 2011916529

Published in the United States of America

10 9 8 7 6 5 4 3 2 1

Notice: The information in this book is true and complete to the best of our knowledge. Its purpose is to inform and to entertain. This book is sold with the understanding that the publisher and author are not engaged in presenting an absolute formula -- only insights about people, places, and events. Every effort has been made to make this book as complete and accurate as possible. However, there may be mistakes both in typography and content. The author and Aquila Media Productions disclaim all liability in connection with the use of this book.

Indigos
The Quiet Storm

Created by Nancy Tappe
Written by Kathy Altaras

Aquila Media Productions
Addison, TX

Acknowledgements

Publishing a book is truly a social and communal event. While it may take a village to raise a child, an Indigo certainty, it also takes one to publish a book. Both of us acknowledge and are grateful for the efforts of friends and family who support us in every endeavor. Mere gratitude seems inadequate for this task.

I wish to give thanks and love to the legion of people who have supported me over the years and who have assisted me with my color psychology in a variety of workshops and Tuesday classes: Nancy Weaver, Gail Kelly, Mimi DiMirjian, Barbera McMenamin, Michelenne Crab, Lynda Gudith, Maureen Hesselgrave, Suzann Lennox, Elana Small, Vickie Schipper, Yves and Yvonne Newman, Ann Connelly, Connie Jensen, Karen Stoddard, Beverly and Doug Waterman, Mimi Miller, Lee and Jerry Hoffman, Rosa Avila, Paula Verdu, Cornelius Ford, Wendell Barnett, Sarah O'Neal, Rob Cohan, Gloria King, and Cindy Runyon. Your assistance and time are invaluable and truly appreciated.

Some friends have blurred the lines over time and become family. They have offered friendship, help, and support countless times and in countless ways: Beatrex Quntanna, Barbra Dillenger and Michael Makay, Kathy Guy, Joyce Lavigne, Kirk and Devon Richardson, Pax Nidorf, Helga Desmet Merz and Hans Juergen Merz, Madelynne and Jerry Helgeson and their son Matthew, and Lyliane Hirtz. Thanks also to Deirdre Morgan for her insights and wisdom.

A special thank you to West and Johannah Leffingwell, who give to me every day in every way. I am so grateful for their kind and selfless efforts. They are truly blessings in my life.

Thank you, Dorothy Stout, for editorial assistance and for your young eyes which bring clarity and corrections to writing and thinking flaws. Terry Berg, thank you for passing along stories from class; they brought strong additions to the text. Thanks also to Andrew Evans, who reminded me of everything about writing that I had forgotten.

Family members have also played a valuable role in bringing these materials to the public. Their support behind the scenes is remarkable and invaluable. Thank you to Laura and Colin Tappe and to David Altaras, who brings more than his share to every partnership and endeavor.

It would be remiss not to mention eternal gratitude to a few people whose support and friendship never wavered, and although they have gone on before us, their devotion to Nancy and her color theories still are special and unforgotten. They are Valdene Vanote, Lis Mahon, Dacia St. John, Gail Samuels, Harriet Pellar, and Glady Griswold.

Inevitably there are those who were inadvertently overlooked. Please know that the mistake is regrettably ours.

Finally, and especially important, thank you to Indigos in our lives who keep us focused on the task at hand and real in our lives and our responses. It is an honor to share time with you. Thank you, Amanda, one of the first and most honest Indigos, for you willingness to let us put some of your more outrageous incidents into print.

Contents

I   Nancy Tappe and Indigo...1

II   The Myth..9

III Meet Some Indigos..17

IV Humanists – One World, One People.....................33

V   Artists – Animated Performers................................41

VI Conceptualists – The Think Tank...........................49

VII Catalysts–The Visionaries..55

VIII Raising Indigo Children, Being Indigo Parents.............61

IX Indigo Students, Indigo Teachers...........................77

X   Indigos at Work...95

XI Love, Indigo Style..103

XII To Indigos Today and Tomorrow.........................109

1

Nancy Tappe and *Indigo*

storm is a confluence of energy moving through the atmosphere to bring about change. On earth, storms occur as part of nature; man can neither halt nor prevent them. Man can only wait them out and then determine a course of action, either using his resources to adjust and adapt to new circumstances or to behave as a hapless victim. In the aftermath of a storm, rebirth and renewal can occur. The fact that mankind is still here today constitutes evidence that he has remarkable talents in courage and adaptation. During the mid-twentieth century, Nancy Tappe saw the beginning of a change that would affect mankind and signal the beginning of a new way of life. She did not recognize it as such initially. No one could have. But she saw it nevertheless, labeled it, and waited to see what would happen.

Nancy Ann Tappe was born in 1932, the daughter of a West Virginia coal mining engineer who struggled to make a living at a time when unions were trying to unite miners. Nancy was the seventh of thirteen children and the only one raised by her Scottish grandparents who accepted and nurtured her odd talents and abilities. She spent her youth in an environment of Scottish mysticism. Today Nancy's language and philosophy still often reflect that early training. A more detailed biography of her life and background appear in two of Nancy's books, *Understanding Your Life through Color*, and *Understanding Your Life through Awareness*.

When Nancy was twelve years old, her grandmother took her to a doctor who diagnosed her with synesthesia, a condition of joined sensations in which an external stimulus is experienced by two (or occasionally more) senses simultaneously. At that time, few people, including doctors, even knew of its existence. Nancy does not recall any further explanation, and her grandparents did not make much of the information. Her grandmother had the same thing; to her there was nothing unusual about Nancy's abilities.

Synesthesia is a physical experience of the brain, not a product of the imagination. The condition is a genetic trait, thought to be a dominant product of the x-chromosome link. Scientists themselves, who write about synesthesia, choose their words carefully. It is not a disease or disorder, nor is it a medical condition. *Trait* seems to be the most accurate descriptor. Although there are many types of synesthesia, the most common form is a visual link between colors and letters of the alphabet, known as grapheme synesthesia. One possessing this form would possibly look at the letter *P*, for example, and always see *P* as blue. Nancy does recall having difficulty learning to read, not really mastering the skill until age eight. Today scientists know that children with color grapheme synesthesia who see color around letters or numbers can have difficulties with reading or math because of the additional visual input.

Another fairly common form is a cross between color and hearing perception. These people experience a marriage of colors and musical tones or keys. The music they hear has color attached, and simultaneously, the colors they hear have sound sensations at the same time. These sensations may be harmonious or discordant.

In Nancy's case, she combines visual color and geometric taste. Nancy sees a variety of colors around every living thing, and most foods have a geometrical shape attached to the regular flavor. This is one of the rarer synesthetic combinations. She has never been without the sensations and frequently wonders what the rest of the world sees or what foods taste like without having shapes attached to them. For example, avocados have an additional pleasant sensation of circles as opposed to macaroni and cheese with its sharp, angular result which causes actual, physical pain. Again, Nancy's sensory perceptions related to synesthesia are described more fully in her other works. Interested readers can also find out many fascinating things about this genetic trait through Internet research.

For the purpose of this book we will only focus on Nancy's synesthetic work with color. Synesthesia was largely unknown during most of Nancy's life. Her grandmother had trained her not to advertise her unusual perceptions or abilities. But when she was twenty-seven, Nancy began a yoga class where the instructor asked everyone to look into a mirror to find a field of energy around themselves. Nancy responded positively; the room danced with color as it always did. The yoga instructor encouraged her to acknowledge her gifts and develop them. And so she soon began years of study categorizing what she saw into patterns and realizing that the patterns had meaning.

Nancy learned what each color signified and how to interpret the different combinations. In general, Nancy sees nine to thirteen colors around a person at all times. Over a lifetime the colors will change in width and intensity, depending on the environment and circumstances of that person's life. One color, however, remains the same throughout the person's life. Nancy calls it the "cradle to grave" color, or life color, which determines the focus of that person's life.

Over time, it became increasingly important to Nancy to find a means to test her information and to organize it into further structure. She contacted a psychiatrist in San Diego, thus beginning five years of working with hundreds of patients and volunteers to define, clarify, and systematize her work. She also began to teach overflowing classes at San Diego State University in the experimental college. One of her most rewarding memories of that period was the opportunity to work with color theorist, Faber Birren (1900-1988.)

Eventually a system of eleven (originally) life colors emerged. Nancy determined that these colors related to the human personality. The colors were hierarchical in nature and followed the color spectrum: magenta, red, pink, orange, lavender, tan, yellow, green, blue, and violet. She also saw some individuals with no color at all, whom she called no-color. Later, on the advice of a gemologist friend, she amended that label to crystal, simply as a vocabulary preference.

For years, Nancy worked as an administrative assistant during the day and then counseled friends and clients at night as she continued clarifying her system. In the early 1970's, she quit her secretarial job and began counseling full time, utilizing her color information. It was also during the early 1970's that she added a twelfth life color, one she called Indigo. She had noticed this color in the late 60's but saw so few of them that she was not sure what it meant. But by the 1970's she saw the numbers begin to increase and added it as a life color.

On the color spectrum Indigo falls between blue and violet. For those readers who like specifics, Nancy identifies indigo in the Red/Green/Blue system as RGB 60 / 22/ 143. In the CMYK system, she sees indigo as 93%, 100%, 4%, 3%. Since no two people see color exactly the same, these numbers indicate only Nancy's perception of the color indigo. It is important to remember that not only do no two people see exactly the same color, but no two synesthetes have exactly the same sensory perceptions.

Nancy's clients represented people with all life colors, and they came from all walks of life. Her color system is outlined fully in *Understanding Your Life through Color*. A delineation of her whole color system is, once again, not the purpose of this book. *Indigos* focuses solely on those individuals who started to appear in the late 1960's and early 1970's and continued to appear in increasing numbers until today, where they account for 95% of the population under ten years old. How and why this population phenomena occurred is at the heart of this book, as is an explanation of the Indigo personality in Nancy's system. This basic primer is the first in a series of materials Nancy will publish about Indigos and their lives.

In reality, the color indigo circled the globe as early as the 60's, perhaps presaging the coming of the new children. Indigo is the dye used to make denim, and jeans are now worn in every country by male and female, old and young, around the globe. The use of indigo dye itself is centuries old.

Within the Indigo life color, Nancy further identified four types of *Indigos:* Humanist, Artist, Conceptualist, and Catalyst. Humanists outnumber the other three significantly, and very few Catalysts have been born yet. A complete chapter in this book will be devoted to each type with the definition and characteristics given. This phenomenon is happening in every culture around the world.

Eventually, according to Nancy's color perceptions from her synesthesia, Indigos will replace all other life colors and will represent the entire range of human experience.

Is there a danger of stereotyping individuals with a labeling system? Yes, of course. But a system of classification allows its creator to define and characterize the commonalities from one category to another as well as the differences. The other danger is one of generalization. Nancy has always realized that individuals are unique -- products of their environment as well as their DNA. The nine to thirteen colors she sees with each person define and describe their uniqueness to her. Consequently to limit the confines of this book to only one of the colors requires generalizations that will leave some readers dissatisfied.

Because Nancy is from the United States, most of her life experience has occurred there. At one time she lived in Asia, and she has spent some of the happiest times of her life in Switzerland. But the vast majority of her observations of the personality patterns from all the life colors are Western. A self-described CNN "junkie" for years, however, Nancy also has observed children throughout the world in all cultures so she is well-versed in percentages worldwide and in the general Indigo pattern. The information in this book applies to Indigos around the world. But she is very aware that changing times in other cultures will affect how Indigos make their mark on that culture. A good example of this is in China, where for the last few decades parents have had to limit their offspring to one child in order to have access for that child to an education, health care, and other social considerations. Today males outrank females by nearly thirty million. How Indigos affect change in Asia can and will be slightly different than how Indigos bring about change in Western cultures. There is no doubt, however, that change in China is occurring even more rapidly than anywhere else on earth.

Today in China over 350 million young people (roughly the current population of the United States) microblog, (the Chinese version of Twitter). Over eighty percent of those are under thirty years of age. They blog for emotional self-expression, sharing of information and ideas, relaxing, learning the status of friends, and researching. They use their social networking capabilities to seek social justice and greater government accountability. Young Chinese spread their concerns about public safety and about job availability. They exert a significant wave of public opinion, and Chinese government officials are forced to listen and to make changes.

Political instability is no deterrent to the development of the Indigo pattern either. The Indigo life purpose is to bring about one world, one people. Children in Somalia, for example, one of the most oppressed nations on earth, are making their mark too. Simply the announcement of their suffering through photos posted around the world enables them to make their presence known and addressed. Developing countries are making the most rapid evolutionary changes, whether those changes happen internally in a peaceful fashion or whether they are externally forced on them by world humanitarian and political pressures.

In other parts of the world, Indigo energy manifests itself by groups in the so-called Twitter Rebellions. These storms are political and dramatic, sweeping away tyrannical regimes (so far) in Tunisia, Egypt, Libya, Kyrgyzstan, and Myanmar. In these popular uprisings, Indigos on cell phones used social media to connect, rebel, and free themselves from outworn, outdated political shackles. No single Indigo led these rebellions; many worked together to spread the word. They used media and technology to give instantaneous information and feedback regarding those countries' leaders and their actions.

Indigos are already receiving honors and acknowledgement for their efforts. One of three women who shared the 2011 Nobel Peace Prize is an Indigo Artist. Tawakkul Karman, a Yemeni journalist, received the honor for her continued non-violent struggle for women's rights and for building peace. As an activist and advocate of human rights, Karman has led protests and rallies for many causes within her country.

Nancy had not the slightest idea that her Indigo label would circle the globe, creating a veritable storm of influence, opinion, believers, naysayers, and self-styled gurus. Nancy Tappe has never seen herself as a guru. Her work with color is a cherished gift she uses to help herself and others to achieve a new awareness of themselves, their friends, and their loved ones. She is constantly excited and fascinated to witness the truths of the human personality and to see similarities shared among individuals.

2

The Myth

As stated in the first chapter, Nancy began teaching seminars and workshops as early as the 1970's, relating her color theories as a synesthete and helping others to understand the human personality as she saw and described it. Her work involved all twelve life colors and the behavior and personality characteristics of each type. Nancy's thought and language are the language of color. By the mid-70's, she began talking about the new Indigos but still focused her work on the entire range of life colors since her audience consisted of people with all colors. In 1986, she wrote *Understanding Your Life thru Color*, a personal account of herself as a synesthete and a definition of her color system. In that book, she briefly described the Indigos and addressed the influence they would have some day. In 2009 this book was reissued as *Understanding Your Life through Color,* 2nd edition, with some additional information about Indigos.

However, Nancy initially declined to promote herself or to give further information because Indigos were still children with undeveloped personalities which were not yet evident to her. She steadfastly refused to guess or make inferences about the Indigos until she saw their life color in greater numbers and until their personality and behavior patterns became clearer to her. It had taken her years to learn the patterns of the other colors. She had initially spent thousands of hours in observation of the first eleven life colors and their habitual behavior, interviewing them in depth about their lives so she could determine firsthand how their life events played out in the aura and in the colors she saw.

However, other people who had either taken her workshops or who had heard of her discussions about this new life color began spreading the word about Indigos in their own teaching and eventually in print.

In many ways, the emergence of Indigos was like birthing a new baby -- slow, painful, and laborious. It was strange not only for us, those already in the world with other life colors in Nancy's color system, but for the early Indigos as well. According to Nancy, their task is to bring about a world that has never existed before, but they themselves did not come in with packaging directions or a detailed syllabus. Early Indigos felt strange at being in unfamiliar surroundings, much like the literal birth process. Some did not like it and changed their color to Blue or Violet. Some did not stay. Some, however, just went along with the flow, different and not always appreciated by those who expected them to be magical, special children. Now, forty years into the process, many of the older Indigos have a sense that their life has not been as easy or special as they were once led to believe.

As decades passed Nancy's reluctance to speak had a downside as well. In her silence, a storm of misinformation and misinterpretation grew, much like Pinocchio's nose. *Indigo children* became a term, a phenomenon, and, for some, a livelihood. Many adults (not Indigos themselves) began to assist Indigo children with their adjustment process. But the lack of available and thorough information during that time caused hypothesis to be delivered as truth. Nancy's synesthetic interpretation of Indigo children within a range of color perceptions and vibrations became lost. An Internet search for *Indigos* or *Indigo children* can turn up an abundance of self-proclaimed experts in the field. Many professionals asserted that they can identify Indigos or that they had taught themselves to identify Indigos. Today there are even supposed tests online to help an individual ascertain whether or not he or she is Indigo.

However, logic defies this process. Nancy's definition of an Indigo individual is completely based on her color perception as a synesthete. Unless a person is identified by Nancy either in person or by photo, a process which she worked out over several decades, no one could actually know for sure what his life color is. Even another synesthete will not perceive things the same way. This author knew of another visual synesthete with a strongly developed sense of color. Where I have one color identity in Nancy Tappe's system, I had a completely different one for the second person, with no overlap at all. No synesthete's sensory information is ever exactly the same, so no one can possibly manifest Nancy's exact perceptions. When she is gone, no one will ever have her synesthetic perceptions until another individual comes along and develops an accurate information system based on his own sensory input and is willing to test and develop his or her information as methodically as Nancy did.

Today, in late 2011, the process of identifying an Indigo is easier. Most Indigos can be identified simply by the math. In the late 1960's, there were very few Indigos born, perhaps one in 5,000. For someone other than Nancy to have claimed the ability to label someone as Indigo would have been highly improbable. By the 1970's, the number increased somewhat. In the 80's, and 90's, Indigo children were born in increasing percentages and in all countries of the world. Today 95% of all children around the world under ten are Indigo, vastly increasing the probability of an accurate self-identification. In addition, with only four, clear sub-categories of Indigo, self-identification is more likely to be accurate than previous ages with twelve colors (in Nancy's system) to choose from. Those with a dual color have a greater challenge to identify themselves accurately, but because Indigos do not blend types, they still have a fairly good chance of determining their subcategories. The most common errors are those who believe they are Catalysts. Nancy herself has only identified fewer than fifty.

Parents of Indigo children can observe personality traits of their children from an early age, so many can guess accurately. But the science is still inexact. Naysayers abound, and for good reason. Synesthesia and a synesthete's sensory impressions are new science, even though it was named and identified in the 1800's. Scientists are beginning to publish more widely about the process itself and about the race to find the genetic links related to this fascinating condition. Publications from syesthetes themselves about their experience are almost non-existent as are accounts of synesthetes who developed their senses into an entire system of meaning. Most synesthetes today still do not publicize their experiences because of how others perceive them. Some synesthetes do not even realize their sensations are different from everyone else.

Part of our message and intent in this book is to provide enough additional information about the Indigo identity and purpose to encourage the many professionals throughout the world who love working with Indigos to do so with more accurate information. Too many Indigos are frustrated and often angry that they themselves don't measure up to the hype about them, nor do they see themselves able to deliver the myth.

What exactly is the myth then? According to public perception in the New Age field, *all Indigo children are magical, psychic, spiritual, wide-eyed creatures who have come to enlighten the world.* Okay, Indigos do seem to be clear-eyed and happy their first few years.

The term "magical" causes a few more problems in interpretation. If Indigos exist in every place on earth, how can they be magical in America or Europe, yet magical in someplace like Somalia at the same time?

According to recent statistics, nearly 1/2 of the world population is under age 25, and 1.2 billion are under age 15. The percentage of Indigo children in the 1.2 billion range is 75%. All of them are not magical, gifted children. In addition, 85% of children in the 1.2 billion range are in developing countries. Yes, they are Indigo. Yes, they have come to show us the future. But the future of Somalia is not the future of America. Indigos in Somalia *are* taking on the enormous spiritual sacrifice of showing the world how and where change is needed. They are magical in their spiritual task. But to announce to the world that all Indigos require private schools and a non-mucous diet, as many assert, is naive and ignores the numbers of Indigos inhabiting the planet, nor is it an effective way to help Indigos understand themselves.

Then what exactly is their magic? Simply put, it's technology, connection, globalization, and communication. Indigos are here to globalize the planet through technology, through global communication systems, and through their desire to be interconnected to one another. They are here to bring about one world. They have created a storm of influence, leading from within rather than by a specific political or religious platform. They show us a global future where individuals are connected through technology, through common interests, and through a disregard for outmoded ways of thinking.

What about the term "psychic?" Yes, all Indigos are intuitive. Some are psychic. A few psychic individuals have been born in every era since time began. There is no data or observation on Nancy's part to suggest that there are more psychic children today than at any other time in history. That said, however, everyone is more aware now than they were fifty years ago.

In addition, there does seem to be an Indigo fascination with superheroes and other world beings. This can be seen in movies, increasing numbers of paranormal shows on TV, the emergence of graphic novels and other art forms with superpowers, etc. There is no doubt that transformation is occurring, and the arts and literature are usually predictive of this. But it is impossible to separate out whether Violets and Indigos caused this interest because of their character, or this is part of the human evolutionary process on our planet at this time. It is likely a combination of both.

Are Indigos spiritual? Of course, but only in the sense that all humans are spiritual at some level. The Indigo purpose is to show us tomorrow and to enjoy today without interference from others. They are the bridge to the future. They are not, however, the future. Another color will emerge, and this group will *be* the future. This will probably not happen in Nancy's lifetime. But she strongly feels that someone else will be alive someday who will be able to identify them and their task. In Nancy's words, "the new color's mission will be to take us on a new adventure in the laws of spirituality and acceptance of all humans equally." Nancy has not seen the advent of any individuals with a new color but acknowledges that according to the logic of the color spectrum, it may be in the ultra-violet range.

Humans view spirituality in subjective terms. Laws of a life on earth call for good and bad, the dark and the light. It is human nature to judge others on their performance throughout their lives, often even to the point of determining what will happen to them after they die. This is a big part of our cultural and religious training, no matter where we are born. Indigos are and will be part of this experience. There are Indigos who are creating heaven on earth. Watch some of the new child prodigies, Indigos who have seemingly arrived with their talents fully developed, unlike anything humans have ever seen before. These children will be discussed more thoroughly in the next chapter.

But there are also Indigos who are creating hell on earth. Some Indigos are failing at their task, and their failure is LOUD. Many of us are shocked at the way they choose to demonstrate what tomorrow looks like. A dramatic example of this was Michael Jackson, a Violet with Indigo aspects. As one of the earliest to demonstrate Indigo energies, he literally was never able to get comfortable in his own skin. He had many Indigo characteristics: his genius was recognized when he was a child, he connected millions of people through his music, and he broke many social traditions. He had an active mind and many intellectual interests. But he was unable to live with who he was, and most people were unable to live with the way he was as well.

Indigos shock in other ways as well. Their industrial strength use of profanity is overwhelming and offensive to most people in prior generations. It fills their daily language, their song lyrics, and their writing. In other outrageous examples of rule-breaking, some Indigos have divorced their parents in public court. Some have shot other children in schools. In Africa, children have become child soldiers, killing one another seemingly at random and for no reason other than the fact that their rebel leader (also Indigo) wants them to. Indigos represent the entire range of human experience, both positive and negative.

Certainly one of the most shocking trends with the Indigos relates to sex. According to recent statistics, 95% of young people today learn about sex from porn on the Internet and television. "Sexting" (sending sexual words and images via cell phones) and group sex are becoming more popularized and prevalent. What they can do is alarming, especially to those of us who were raised with different moral and cultural values. *Don't ask; don't tell* was the norm for centuries. To repress mankind's animal tendencies has been the moral message throughout all religions and time. Indigos appear to be throwing that in our faces. But who is to say that mankind does not need shock value to get the message at this point in our evolution? How do we as humans judge another person's spiritual task when we do not exactly know what that spiritual task is or what humans need to evolve further?

A final segment of the Indigo children mythology in New Age theory relates to crystal children. Again literature of all kinds abounds. Crystal children are described as another group of children with special talents and abilities. Has Nancy ever seen this group?

Yes and no. Nancy used to define crystal as one of the colors in her synesthetic range of twelve life colors. This color spectrum is a hierarchy of learning and spiritual progression with magenta and red at the bottom of the spectrum, people whose focus is physical existence and experience. Blue and Violet were at the top end of the life color spectrum, those individuals who are more creative and spiritual in their life task. Crystals were graduates who came here to assist others in their progression. There was nothing magical, psychic, or special about their abilities. They stopped being born in the mid-20th century because their task was no longer needed. Nancy has seen no crystals born since then, nor has she ever seen another group of children with some special spiritual purpose. However, some of the crystals born many years ago are now beginning to work more closely with Indigos, a clear sign that many Indigos are struggling and need help. In that respect, Nancy acknowledges that it is possible for some crystal babies to be born in the next few years to assist the Indigos as well. They are not, and will not, be another "magical group of children here to help the planet" in any other sense than they have been before.

The term "New Age" itself is really yesterday's news as it relates to Indigos and their lives today. Indigos are all already aware that they are different. They are already showing us rapid globalization, dramatic changes in behavior, and the human need to be interconnected with others. New Age philosophy was dreamy, idealistic, and abstract. The Indigos have moved on.

Since Nancy began teaching and working with the term *Indigo* in the 70's, the concept has become globally recognized. Graduate students in

Russia have contacted her regarding their theses and doctoral dissertations on the subject. Publishers in Europe and Asia have published her views on the Indigo development, as have media representatives from radio and television. A number of authors have written about Indigos, and today a wide range of books, articles, and websites exist about them. Hundreds of adults have focused all or part of their professional lives around assisting young Indigos in school and in their relationships.

Did Indigos create the technological age? No, Violets did. Indigos have simply sped it along and shown the rest of us how powerful and useful technology is as a tool that can affect every aspect of our lives. It is difficult to separate cause and effect or to discuss one color in isolation from the others.

Will the Indigo storm influence and change the planet? Definitely yes and in every aspect of the human experience. The remainder of this book is Nancy's attempt to clarify the label and personality patterns she identified over forty years ago and put to rest the fantasy and science fiction that have emerged since then. Nancy's subsequent materials will give Indigos themselves further guidelines in their work and their relationships and will give those with other life colors in Nancy's system greater understanding of young Indigos and their work for the future.

Indigos have had a sweeping affect on the world in their first forty short years on the planet. But to focus on them as a collective would be to miss the best part, the Indigo person.

3

Meet Some Indigos

*I*magine yourself in an ordinary, college classroom today. Professor Albright is at the front, showing slides in a darkened theater-style lecture hall. His lecture lasts most of an hour and is delivered in a monotone with little notice of whether his students are attentive or not. Students are spread throughout the auditorium. Most have laptops or tablets for note-taking. Other than the new technology and perhaps theater-style seating, it is a scene that has taken place around the world for hundreds of years. Nothing new here.

But in the class are Indigos, students who multi-task effortlessly, who were raised on a rapid array of sound, words, and images per second via television and video games, and who do not feel compelled to pay attention. They are there; that should be enough. They'll pass the test. How they choose to master the material, or if they choose to master it, is up to them.

Let's meet some of them.

Blake sits at one side, slightly hung over. He is college age, likes the social life at school but has no specific major and has not taken a class yet that really "hooked" him into taking more like it. He has thought repeatedly about dropping out but has promised his parents to complete the semester. Blake has not purchased the text yet, but he is beginning to see that he probably should. He signs on to the Internet, navigates to his favorite online bookstore, purchases and downloads the text, and while he is there anyway, decides to purchase and download a couple of songs. He has really been wanting to get one of them. He puts in his ear buds and begins to listen as soon as it is ready. At the same time he receives and sends three texts about meeting some friends for coffee later in the afternoon. Blake checks to make sure the professor posted his notes online and decides to keep listening to his music.

Across the room are roommates Mahima and Xia. They are not seated together because Xia arrived late. There is no need. They are backchanneling -- listening to the lecture but texting and emailing each other across the room while the professor speaks. Xia sends two photos via her phone from last night's party. Mahima accesses one of the images from the lecture and emails it to Xia for an upcoming project they are working on together. They like the class and look forward to the project. Mahima goes online again to check her bank balance.

Behind them is Emma, working to finish a paper due in two hours for another class. She still has a long way to go. While she tries to pull her thoughts together, she checks in with one of her online games to see who has played recently. Emma has already accessed the university site to make sure the professor for this class posted his lecture. She'll listen to the podcast later.

While the above scenario is contrived, it illustrates many general Indigo characteristics. To begin with, the Indigo mind processes sensory information at lightning speed. Indigos can assimilate, process, store, retrieve, and remember data faster than at any time in history. A positive side to this is their ability to multi-task, behavior that is annoying for many non-Indigos. It is important for others to realize that when you call or email Indigos, they may be playing a game online, chatting with friends in one or more chat sites, answering email, doing homework, and making a video of their weekend activities -- all simultaneously. Music will be blasting in the background, and the TV may be on as well. They do not see this behavior as anything extraordinary. It is just what they do. In addition, they do not view their gadgets as toys or luxuries. Their cell phones, tablets, laptops, and game devices are extensions of themselves. If they felt like it, they could easily defend their having these devices and their constant use. Students can articulate what they like about their games and can talk about the kinds of skills and creativity they gain from their constant use. Many Indigos report appreciating real-world feedback from their blogging or hobby chat sites. Even when someone disagrees with their opinion, Indigos feel that it has greater authenticity than getting a grade on a paper where the teacher just wrote, "good job," or "keep up the good work." Others like the ability that some games such as World of Warcraft allow them in social innovation, problem solving, creativity, or extended involvement with a single focus. They use their devices to "veg out" the way our generation uses television.

To outsiders, however, Indigos look unfocused, hyperactive, and from their perspective, just downright rude as they sneak glances at incoming texts, emails, or chat room socializing. Perspective is the right word though. Indigos do not believe they are being rude. They are just processing multiple kinds of input and information much faster than we are. And for them, some channels of information come in so slowly or are so lacking in context for the Indigo purpose, that Indigos just move on inside their head. They tune out who, what, and where they are, causing them to look even less focused to outsiders.

What has happened then is that parents, teachers, professional educators, and psychologists have labeled the Indigo *lacking* in ability to process information in the old way. The most popular labels are ADD or Attention Deficit Disorder, or ADHD or Attention Deficit Hyperactive Disorder. What these labels mean are that yesterday's and today's professionals call the speed at which many Indigos process information a *disorder* and, sadly, have determined it to be wrong. They have a *deficit* or a *disorder* because they cannot process information according to old, standardized norms of yesterday. Yes, many Indigos are deficient at slowing down to process information in the only way most of the rest of us put information out. Indigos think and move faster. Nor do they lack focus. All it takes to question this diagnosis is to watch an Indigo's focus and determination as he plays a video game for several hours or even all night, seldom moving from his bed, chair, or computer.

Nancy Tappe believes this behavior is not wrong and Indigos are not unfocused. It is largely an issue of how Indigos use TIME. The Indigo mind moves in a faster time and at a faster pace. It sorts and assigns value to which input it will need for the future. Unfortunately, today's Indigos still live in an authority world created by non-Indigos. And they are judged accordingly. Many children in the last four decades have been put on medication to slow them down to their parents', teachers', or schools' time frame. This issue will be discussed more thoroughly in Chapter 9, Indigo Students, Indigo Teachers.

A second characteristic of Indigo behavior and thinking, then, is related to the first. Blake, Mahima, Xia, and Emma do not think they are being rude to Professor Albright during his lecture, nor do the Indigos just discussed (those labeled as ADD or ADHD) intend rudeness. They have an inner sense of entitlement that enables them to consider their point of view right. After all, Professor Albright's lecture materials will be immediately accessible online. In person, he is slow, boring, and hidden behind his projector. He makes no attempt to engage them; why should they fake a response they don't feel? If other parents, teachers, or psychologists have a value system that is not shared nor endorsed by the Indigo, who cares? There is no intended defiance. They dislike rules for the sake of rules and disregard authority simply because of age or position. They feel they are equal and should be treated equally. They are brilliant with a wise understanding about humanity and are uncanny and accurate judges of character. They read what you *do*, not what you say, and then they react accordingly. They feel that their entitlement is earned, and they cannot be made to feel guilty about expressing it. They do not fake their feelings just for the sake of polite social conventions that have no inherent value. In addition, they see through hypocrisy and tune out any adult they do not respect. Their entitlement, then, is their version of integrity, of being true to their own internal value system rather than a social facade made in another time.

The truth is that all of us in generations before the Indigos also thought the hypothetical Professor Albright was boring. We also wished we were listening to our music or whatever the leisure activity of the day was. And we all knew that Professor Albright did not care who we were either. He had the power; we had to be there and listen. The great difference between the other life colors and the new Indigo is that they *do* what we always *thought*. We were culturally trained into a behavior that we did not want in a system we did not challenge. Indigos *own* their thoughts and their behavior, willing to challenge every system in front of them. They bring their storms right into the lecture hall, breaking down assumptions about correct behavior that have existed in education for over a thousand years, and they are doing it without hesitation or remorse.

Another fascinating cultural change that Indigos are making is reflected in the ratio of boys to girls in the vignette at the beginning of this chapter. Today females outnumber males in nearly all colleges. This trend begins in high school and continues through professional school and into professions. Today more young women than men are entering (and graduating) from medical school, dental and law schools, engineering schools, and many of the technical fields. In some colleges, the male / female ratio is so imbalanced that admissions officials are afraid girls won't apply to those schools because there are too many girls and too few boys. This disparity has interesting ramifications, including the appearance of books in the marketplace about *what's wrong with young men today and what do educators need to do to force boys to stay in school?* Again, modern culture is making the philosophical determination that Indigo males are lacking something -- drive, motivation, gumption, determination. There is a huge difference between observing change and judging change. On the one hand, boys are shaking up the education system with their escalating drop-out rates. Some create havoc by openly boasting about sabotaging standardized tests; others simply drop out and move on.

Nancy looks at it differently. In the 1960's one of the characteristics Nancy labeled as Indigo was that they would be more androgynous. That is exactly what happened. Most people who heard this were not surprised to see both boys and girls move to an era where everyone wore jeans, T-shirts, and long hair styles. From behind, it was difficult to tell a male from a female. But Nancy's meaning and intent went far beyond attire. Indigo *energy* itself is becoming androgynous, more interchangeable. Young Indigo men are taking on homemaking and child-rearing tasks while women are much more comfortable climbing their way up the career ladder, earning the larger salary, and pursuing continued education. Our cultural perception since time began is that male energy should dominate, and female energy should not. THAT is what is changing. What a giant shift! There is nothing wrong with Indigo males who want to stay home, who discontinue their formal education for awhile, or who seemingly lack purpose. There is nothing wrong with Indigo females becoming the breadwinner, managing the family finances, or climbing the corporate ladder. It is our cultural perception of what is wrong or right that needs to change. Young Indigo fathers share child-care responsibilities equally. They clean, cook, or do laundry for the sake of time management or efficiency in running the house. Females share financial management, auto repair, or maintenance tasks equally. Every-one works together for the good of the whole. Traditional roles mean little to the Indigo. They work side by side to establish and maintain the lifestyle they like best.

As outsiders (those of us who are older or who do not have Indigo life colors,) it is time to reevaluate our beliefs and our perceptions of what is culturally acceptable. At the least, we can start to observe and appreciate the rapid social changes that Indigos are making.

To be sure, Indigos feel the effects of this androgynous energy themselves. They were born in a world with parents and grandparents who had well-defined gender roles. The environment for early Indigo children was structured, defined, and expectations were pretty clear. The early myth of "those special, evolved beings" ran smack into reality when the Indigo patterns began to solidify and Indigo teens and young adults began to exert their ideas and opinions. Indigos were often un-easy even with themselves. Many are in obvious conflict with people they love, their parents. Many feel they have let down those who trusted them and who had bright hopes for their future.

The difficulty is that the Indigo has an internal value system with a different agenda. Many are still uncertain about their future. Some of the older Indigos who have already defined their career goals may change their field of work completely over the next few years as Indigo energies continue to change our world. Their great challenge is that they led the way with an incomplete roadmap. As they fill in the gap, they are finding roads that are incomplete, unpaved, and full of potholes. Many continue to live at home until they are thirty years old. In the last fifteen years Indigos have been restless and often angry at their perceptions of the world, at knowing they don't fit in and not knowing why, and at not being able to do much about it. Previous generations have always been taught to follow the rules of yesterday; Indigos have a cellular structure that wants to leap into tomorrow. Today, they are waiting impatiently to see what their future holds. They want to create new structures, but are restless and angry as old structures demand time to be torn down. They see their elders living in a culture where hypocrisy is standard, "old boy" mentality still rules in many places, and where people in charge rule through guilt or intimidation. Indigos just aren't into that. They look at the world objectively and impersonally, take in what they need, and then move on.

What the message should be is that it is acceptable and understandable for them to feel uncertain of their purpose, unclear as to their future, and unaware of the reasons behind their confusion. They will be late bloomers. The bulb is in the ground; it just isn't spring yet. That is certainly much easier said than done though. Some have been pushed by teachers, parents, or other authority figures into directions they don't see for themselves or want to become. Playing out uncertainty year after year while living with one's parents has caused some Indigos to become addicted to the violence of computer games. Some have carried this violence into real life. Some do nothing, living at home and drifting through each day without focus or meaning. In a sense, these early Indigos were like sprinters who leap before the gun has gone off -- false starters who have to regroup and begin again.

The most successful Indigos in today's world are those who acknowledged at some level that they had to adjust to a society that wasn't quite ready for them. They were willing to compromise their attitudes, reactions to old norms, and expectations of what their life would be like in order to get along. Some have traveled or dedicated time to service to others abroad. Others have stayed in school, drifting from one field of study to another. Many have just gotten a job, content to hang out until they stumble into a future that feels right to them.

Most Indigos find solace in their friendships. Notice in the vignette that all of them spent at least a few minutes during the class period checking in with friends for a variety of purposes. As indicated in the previous chapter, Indigos are interconnected. Their social life is their world. Even more important, it is their life task. The Indigo purpose is to create one world where society and culture are global, not national and where individuals live, travel, and work in multiple countries, not multiple town or states within their individual country. All

Indigos do this. They reach out to each other. Each of the four types of Indigo will socialize differently, but all will socialize. While the Humanists are paving the way with their social networking communication systems, the Artists will share their work with others around the world with like interests. Conceptualists in scientific and medical fields already interact daily with colleagues in other countries that they may never meet in person.

Notice also in the vignette that one student was Indian, one Asian, and two were Caucasian of unknown origin. Indigos are creating one world where people travel, study and live in other countries, and interchange ideas and information from all over the world. Indigos will eventually bring about one world, most likely through business and corporate cultures. They will see a time where there is one world currency, one primary language, one governing system for global peacekeeping and earth crisis management. Each country and area will still retain its individuality and heritage, but the primary focus will be cooperative and global. A unified, global world will have the robustness of a business economy but also the changeability and occasional instability. It will not be run by one, all-powerful political factor.

Fast, entitled, androgynous, social, and a little lost, yes, these are Indigo characteristics. What else are they like?

They are the laziest of all the colors in Nancy's spectrum, although they do not regard themselves as lazy. They take their time and do things their way. They are mechanical, operating with an "on" or "off" switch. If they did not flip the switch by themselves, then there is no need to act. Others can't make them. If something is already working, why bother it? Consequently, they need stronger motivation than the rest of us. It is best to find out what they want and then to provide guidance or motivation to get them moving.

Indigos can party hard. They love junk food, junk culture, and junk entertainment. Most seem to tolerate it well, balancing it with their lifestyle. Some, however, addict easily to their music, their games, to the computer in general, or to their social networking. Today, drinking is proliferating for the Indigo. Again, some tolerate it fairly well. In others, it can lead to real problems as they age. Indigos regard both drugs and alcohol as temporary behavior alterations.

Another basic characteristic of the Indigo is his or her natural exuberance. They are naturally joyful. Others call it "hyper" or "overactive" and try to stifle or soften it, preferring restraint to enthusiasm. Indigos own their joy and see no reason for restricting it. Why would anyone want to restrict joy?

Indigos love sign language in whatever their native language. Even those cultures that previously had no provision for the deaf in their society (such as Mongolia) are beginning to develop a common sign language so as to include a segment of the population that, in centuries before, were excluded. It is no mistake that using simple sign language is now common in infant and toddler upbringing.

Another way to approach understanding an Indigo's energy and personality is to look at their new mythology, *Harry Potter*. This wonderful series combined remnants of Christian, Arthurian, Greek, and Roman past traditions and belief systems with space games and superpowers in an environment of friends who understand each other and stick together. Characters in this series did not come from a nuclear family and did not eat dinner at the family table each evening. In the very first chapter of the very first book, Harry moves to Hogwarts, away from an environment that did not nurture or support his special talents. Some elements of these books and movies are especially Indigo: Potter's character and gifts were recognized as a young child; he constantly made decisions based on what he knew was right, even when it meant defying authority; and Potter's saga happened to him while he was young. He used his gifts, both psychic and intellectual, intuitively. To him, they were just tools to be used when necessary. No big deal. At the conclusion of the series as an adult, he chose to live an ordinary life.

Where are Indigos comfortable?

Computers and space games are the favorite Indigo toys, even for girls. Humanists work well with toys that are action figures because they look and can act like people. Conceptualists seem to gravitate toward gaming, focusing on the technical applications it offers and pushing themselves to master and control aspects of each game. They like and excel at war games. Indigo boys today are weapons oriented, a dynamic that has developed from their video games. The girls' weapons are psychological. Martial arts have grown in popularity among many Indigos. They offer young people a place to focus their energies, both physical and mental. Artists like the creativity and design elements of videos, games, and their music.

All Indigos seem to find a favorite genre of music and stick to it. Sub-genres exist that many people don't even know about. Indigos mix and remix their own music creations, sharing them throughout the world with those who have similar tastes.

In Western culture today many Indigos are born or raised by a single parent or by parents who no longer live together. Indigos seem to adapt to this lifestyle well. They enjoy being with the parent of the moment, adjusting to each environment and behavior while they are with that parent and then shifting to the next one as the need arises. Over time and given a choice, however, Indigos will gravitate toward the one with the money. They love their fathers but have a special bond with mother.

Indigos also love their grandparents. Many are being raised by them all or part of the time. Indigos appreciate the love that comes from grandparents, who no longer have parental angst over child rearing. Grandparents offer a safe haven for Indigo youth. Quite often they show a picture of stability that is lacking in the lives of the Indigos' parents. Indigos appreciate and resonate to the stability because they themselves are constantly changing. With their focus on the future, they have little in their lives that demonstrates stability and dependability. While Indigos are clearly here to show us the future, they do not dislike the past. They are willing to share the past with their grandparents and retain family values and memories that link them to what has gone on before them. But they will not live the way of their grandparents, nor will they conform to older values. They prefer to appreciate the past at a distance.

Indigos are nurtured by nature. They do not have to come from rural settings or live on a coastline to find the out of doors healthy for them. Indigos and their friends seek out any place they can to hang out with their friends, be outside, or participate in a casual event to replenish themselves and their bodies. There are some experts in child rearing today who worry about the increased amount of time Indigos spend inside with their technology. However, those Indigos not actively involved in sports still find time and opportunity to hike together, travel to scenic areas, or pursue hobbies like biking, off-roading, or camping.

On the whole, Indigos' greatest comfort comes from informal settings, planning things on the spur of the moment, and hanging out with people they like best -- friends or family.

Where are they uncomfortable? Just as they are happiest in informal settings, they are most uncomfortable in contrived and formal settings, those places and events that are ritualized for the sake of ritual and where they are expected to behave according to someone else's sense of appropriateness. They prefer real to artificial.

Indigos also hate being smothered and are resistant to "gushy" type people or those who are fake in their delivery. They do not like polite, social talk where everyone pretends to be fine and some topics of conversation are completely avoided. Generations prior to the Indigos lived in a "don't ask, don't tell" social structure that applied to all areas of life. People believed that "less is more." The less they knew of people and their issues, the more content they were. Indigos are rapidly changing this mindset. They have a sensitivity that prior generations may have had but were not permitted to express in their social structure. To communicate with Indigos today, you must give them permission to tell you anything they are thinking without shock value on your part. Indigos like straight talk, and they love sharing information. They do not want to be talked down to, and they definitely don't want to be talked "at." They love good conversation; they want the truth, and they want consistency. They like everything out in the open. They do not require that you agree with them, and they are willing to listen to your point of view if you can state it as objectively as they do. You just have to be ready to listen to their expression of who they are. Their communication is clear, honest, and sometimes brutally frank. They are especially sensitive to praise or to criticism.

Cultural conventions of politeness and pretension do not come naturally to the Indigo. Humanists and Artists can endure an artificial conversation longer than the other two types of Indigo, but they will not stay long. Artists like the focus to be about them. Humanists will just seek someone else to talk to. The Conceptualists are the most politically motivated of all four groups. They may stay with a conversation or individual if there is something to gain, and they won't always tell the truth. All Indigos consider themselves equal to whatever generation or socioeconomic level they are with. They do not intimidate easily, and they do not feel guilt associated with environmental pressure. Parents cannot make them feel guilty. Indigos may choose to feel guilt, but that is a personal choice.

Indigos love to be right in the skin of whomever they are with -- connected and paying attention. And conversely, they can get under one's skin faster than anyone. Dealing with them directly just never seems to go quite the way one plans.

Paradoxically, they can also exaggerate and dramatize their storytelling. When they are with people who are tight-lipped or who are not honest and open in their communication, they will communicate the same way, answering briefly, but not really sharing themselves or their information generously. Keys to successful communication with Indigos are listening to them without preconceptions and asking them questions which will allow them to present their views openly. It is essential to listen to them without judgment of any kind, a difficult task for their parents and grandparents, who were raised by another set of rules. It does not seem to occur to the Indigo to be less frank or honest with older generations than they are with each other.

Are Indigos different physically? Yes, in several ways. Indigos regard the skin covering their body as a blank canvas. It is theirs to make their mark on -- literally. They record their personal preferences, history, impulses, and passions by tattooing or piercing some or all body parts. Tattoos enable some to bring color to the world and some to have a new sense of freedom that had customarily been denied to young people before. To many of them, body art is an attempt to define themselves. Today, Nancy feels that many have gone overboard and will someday regret the extent of their enthusiasm. This trend shows little signs of changing, but many young Indigos today will not tattoo themselves to the extent that some of the earlier Indigos did.

Indigos consider their bodies as tools -- easily changed and mechanized. If one part goes bad, then they are willing to put in a new part and get back on the road. Watch young Indigo athletes demonstrate this in action. During an Olympics interval, there is frequent news about today's young people. You can hear news commentators discuss how a participant had surgery within just a few days or weeks of their competition, and yet they are back in action and winning medals.

Indigos are also not in the least hesitant to use cosmetic surgery to enhance their bodies. Buying boobs, a new chin, a more attractive nose, or injectable substances to add volume or fullness to the lips or skin is a necessity for some Indigos who wish to retain their youthfulness or increase their sex appeal. Once they get their body "just right," they may have little incentive to make further changes. As one young newlywed related to his mother, "No, Mom, I don't think we are going to have children. Stephanie doesn't want to mess up her 34C's. I told her I'd buy her some new ones after the baby came, but she doesn't want to risk it."

Another current trend that Nancy has noticed is that many Indigo young adults have knee problems. This seems to be happening to athletes and non-athletes alike. At this time Nancy does not know if this is part of the Indigo pattern or just a current trend.

There are changes inside the body as well. Nancy feels that the physical body in general is beginning to lose its immune system, an indicator of how the human body is evolving to handle change. Indigos demonstrate evidence of this through lowered resistance to viruses and insect bites, bugs both inside and out. This evolutionary change will continue for hundreds of years, but eventually the endocrine system will take the place of the immune system. Indigos appear ready for this process.

Nancy has also observed that many Indigos do seem to have trouble assimilating foods that make mucous in the body. This is usually exhibited in the bronchial areas and can manifest in ear and throat difficulties. Most of these respiratory problems occur before the age of five, after which children seem to be able to acclimate more successfully. However, most children under five today are in pre-school. Many have been there since they were just a few months old. During these years colds, flu, and viruses are passed from one child to another with greater frequency. Current trends indicate that children have fewer colds and viruses once elementary school begins and their own individual immune system builds up a stronger resistance. This pattern is even true of Indigos in Asia, India, or other areas where indigenous diets and environments are completely different.

Within the Indigo range, there are four basic divisions or types: Humanist, Artist, Conceptualist, and Catalyst. Humanists are socializers, the "people people." They use social networking, gaming, work, music, and play to stay connected to their friends and social groups. Artists are intensely creative and dynamic people, often displaying new ideas and techniques with their art, which may be in any field of endeavor. Artists focus on their special interest and may or may not be attached to people unless they share the same interest. They are "drama queens" of the world; their life and its events are always dramatic and often exaggerated. Conceptualists are project people, disciplined and devoted to the project of the moment. People are important to them, but in a focused and directed way; people and relationships can be sacrificed for the good of the project if necessary. And finally, Catalysts are other-worldly, large-bodied, not easily socialized, and often aloof. Nancy has seen few Catalysts so far. They seem to be the last to appear and the least able to acclimate to our world today.

There is no spiritual hierarchy. No one type is more "evolved" than the others. Each type is distinct and brings a different set of talents and abilities according to the needs of time. Today there are fewer Catalysts because old systems are not completely broken down; man is not ready yet for the next step.

These four types represent the entire range of human experience. Humanists have led the way because their goal is to interconnect humanity before the Catalysts bring in new theories and philosophies. Artists and Conceptualists are creating the designs and mechanical processes by which the Catalysts will deliver their message. Each type will be described more thoroughly in the next four chapters.

In addition, there are many Indigos who have two types, as seen in the illustration below. The Humanist / Artist duality is fairly common, as is the Artist / Conceptualist. The diagram below illustrates that within the Indigo life color, there are ten possible combinations: Humanist, Artist, Conceptualist, Catalyst and then six other dual-color combinations: Humanist/Artist, Humanist/Conceptualist, Humanist Catalyst, Artist/ Conceptualist, Artist/Catalyst, and Conceptualist / Catalyst. To a certain extent the dual type Indigos have one asset the pure types do not. When presented with something new, a dual type can examine it through two lenses, not just one.

Indigos with dual colors do not merge or blend their types. When they are in the Humanist mode, they are clearly Humanist. But if they switch to an alternative, such as Artist, then they behave clearly as Artists. There is no specific amount of time they have to be in either mode. The type is a tool; they use it to suit their own internal purpose. However, tool selection is not arbitrary. They are born one or two Indigo types and then seldom change within their lifetime. There are no Indigos with three combinations.

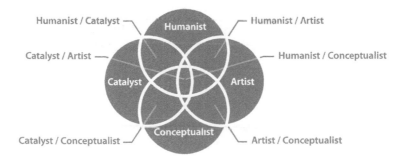

What if you do not know if you are an Indigo? Or what if you do not know which kind? On the whole, it doesn't matter. In fifty years everyone will be Indigo or will add Indigo consciousness to the color they were born with. Everyone is moving into a globalized way of thinking, is adjusting to a faster perception of time, and is integrating technology into every aspect of life. What is important is your ability to see the Indigo commonality: globalized thinking and living, technological savvy, clear and honest communication, and reluctance to buy into outmoded conventions, no matter what your age or where you are from. Do you see these qualities becoming more characteristic of you and your personality? If so, then you are adjusting to Indigo energy.

There is one additional phenomenon that is Indigo in nature but not specifically attached to any one type. Watch today's child prodigies. Most experts today agree that prodigies of the past like Mozart, Jeremy Bentham, or Picasso, who clearly demonstrated genius as children, did so with impressive but unsophisticated talent that they developed slowly over many years. Today's Indigo prodigies come in with their talent fully developed. They show the full range of what is potential here on earth. Some will exemplify the Harry Potter myth -- do their talent when young and then become ordinary. Others may save it until they are older or maintain it their whole lives. It is easy to be flabbergasted by the amazing soprano voice of Jackie Evancho or the spiritual artist Akiane. While many of these geniuses are Indigo Artists, all are not. Today there are Conceptualist prodigies working in technology and other fields

It is impossible to know if there are more prodigies today than in other eras, or whether they are the same in number as they always were, but today's media brings them to a global awareness that was not possible before. In any event, whenever we see one of these brilliant and gifted individuals, we are aware that their talent is very, very impressive. They are, indeed, showing us an exciting future.

4
Humanists – One World, One People

W hat is it? Is it English? Yes, sort of, in a George Orwellian *1984* kind of Newspeak. It is text language, an impoverished phonetic brevity that Indigos use to speed up their communications. Silent e's are gone, as are many vowels. Capital letters are gone as is punctuation unless it is used for emphasis. Numbers and symbols double for homonyms or add even further brevity. It is a thumb language, written by texters writing with both thumbs, definitely faster than the index finger alone. It's fast, it's efficient, and it's the ultimate Indigo tradition buster.

If the reader paid careful attention to the population figures in Chapter Two, then it figures that there are literally millions of young Indigo Humanists on the planet. How, then does one single them out and describe them in a way that makes them identifiable and human? Nancy sees between nine and thirteen colors in a person's aura, only one of which is the life color. The others relate to how a person is introverted or extroverted, the influence of his mother and father, his home life, and how he is perceived by others. All the colors together make up each individual's personality at the present time. And, as mentioned before, some colors fluctuate in intensity or permanence based on how the individual is doing with his life.

The life color dominates the other layers within an individual's aura. The Indigo life color is the only focus of this book. What distinguishes Humanists from other Indigos and other life colors? The reader can look for several clues. First and foremost, Humanists are about people. Their life task is to bring new insights into human relationships and humanity. They are "people people" who can talk to anyone about anything. People are their strength, and humanity is their interest. They have come to help globalize people. As teens and young adults, their peer group is their life. They are the most likely to belong to school or church groups, team sports, music groups, or to use social media easily and fluently. They like being connected to others with similar interests. They are the most enthusiastic in general, and the most outgoing. They literally light up when they are with people they like. When their place and position in the group is secure, they are secure. They do not like to be by themselves, either awake or asleep, and they will take on a solitary activity only when they know someone else is close by.

What do Humanists look like around the world? Meet Anguet, a young woman in Sudan. Born and raised in a traditional Muslim village, Anguet likes and plays volleyball, running around the court in her native garb but making sure her hair is covered at all times. Anguet's mother encourages her enthusiasm and ability, but her father scowls from the stands, uncomfortable that his daughter is showing off in front of men. Traditional women in Sudan do not play sports. Anguet, age 16, also still attends school, another break with social tradition. She wants to become a teacher. When she can, she uses the computer at a local NGO to follow her favorite soccer teams.

Katie lives in Singapore. She is seven years old. Her father is an American who works for a Swiss company. Her mother is German. Katie speaks English and German; she is now learning Chinese in school. She loves sports. No matter where they live or travel, she swims, skis, and plays soccer. Her new best friend is Chinese. Katie Skypes with both grandmothers, one in Germany and the other in Ohio.

Rafael lives in Panama. He has been trained as a naturalist and works in the travel and tourism industry. He meets people from all over the world, giving lectures about the plants and wildlife native to Panama. Outgoing and friendly, Rafael hopes to own his own tourism business some day. He supports his parents and two younger brothers. In his free time, Rafael is a gamer, loving the opportunities his games give him to compete with and against his friends and those he has teamed up with in other countries.

Finally, meet Lou, a small town guy from Georgia. Lou works for a large insurance company. He spends his day in a cubicle, but he is far from isolated. Lou coordinates efforts for his company with workers in New Jersey, London, Sweden, and Tokyo. Lou is not a global traveler, but a few weeks ago he helped organize a group of people from his church to travel to a neighboring state for a long weekend to work with flood relief efforts. He met some new friends that he is eager to keep in touch with.

What do these Indigo Humanists have in common? They are social both in work and in play. They are curious about others and will step outside their comfort zone easily and naturally to experience others. They use computers and other forms of technology to stay connected with people they know and to make new connections with those they do not.

Humanists also stand out because of their temperament. Easy-going and fun-loving, they prefer impulse to habit. They are fun to be with. For them people *are* the event. Hanging out is a favorite activity, even when it extends to dating. The positive side of their personality is cheerful and good-natured. They love to tease others, but they can often carry it too far, especially with those who regard it as being needled. The Humanists regard it as affection and play. They can be cuddlers; even boys will do it in an off-beat, goofy way.

This casual and relaxed attitude extends to the workplace as well. Humanists prefer a relaxed, non-formal approach in their work environment. They can work within the confines of a cubicle, as long as their own is surrounded by many others. They resent long hours and deadlines unless they are working with friends. When looking for a job, the Humanist should ask about and try to observe the culture of the place before signing on. Do the people look friendly? Do they seem to interact with each other? How well do they work together? Are there social functions? Can they put photos of friends and family in their work area? All these factors add up to the humanity of the working environment. That will often determine whether a Humanist likes the job or stays with it.

The 1990's version of Indigo Humanists was the television show *Friends*. Most scenes featured the ensemble group of young adults in New York together in an apartment or a local coffee house. In each episode they helped with each others' problems and shared their joys. Over time they become family, in some cases literally, with two of the couples forming romantic relationships by the end of the series. Plot lines developed via conversation instead of action. Half of the cast members actually were Indigos: Lisa Kudrow, Matt LeBlanc, and David Schwimmer, all Indigo Artists.

Typically Indigos today like to be friends before beginning a relationship. Today's friendships often happen in chat rooms, web groups, and on Facebook. Their cell phone is their lifeline. Humanists view games as an opportunity to interact with others, unlike Conceptualists who like the strategy, competition, and a chance to win. Humanists view technology as the means to be connected to other people.

Think of Humanists as herd animals; they move in groups, graze frequently, and are non-militant. They don't like to stand out -- preferring to lead from within or as part of the group as a whole. One individual can move to the front, but it is from a desire to move in the right direction, not to stand out from the rest. Nancy has observed that the vast majority of the people recently televised in the populist rebellions were Indigo Humanists, all young and all rebelling for the cause of freedom for themselves and those in their environment. Humanists are peace lovers, but they will not run from a fight.

A third indicator of the Humanist is his skill as a direct communicator. The Indigo mission is to teach through talking, writing, or putting their thoughts out for others to see and share. They love to talk, and when they get on a roll, they can talk non-stop. Quieter ones can easily put their thoughts into writing. This quality often propels them into positions of leadership and influence, but again, within the group, not outside it. They work out their thoughts and ideas by sharing them with their friends and talking to others. In the classroom these Indigos prefer group projects or talking things over with a partner. On the job, they prefer working together in teams or in a collegial environment.

Humanists text, blog, and chat, keeping themselves connected to others with words and speech. To be sure, their spelling looks a lot different than ours used to. They are changing language daily, ignoring conventions that have been in place for centuries. And although they claim to know the difference between formal and informal use of language, it is linguistically curious to see what wins out eventually, whether language in general will go through an enormous evolutionary shift like it did in Chaucer's time when Middle English, the language of the streets, overtook Latin and French as the primary format for writing and speaking.

Humanists have a great ability to express themselves orally and to speak extemporaneously, in part, because it is very important for them to prove their point. They do like to get in the last word. Consequently, they are excellent communicators. Good subjects for them in school are foreign language, debate, and speech. They can do impromptu orations, where the other types would be terrified. Most are also good writers as long as they get to choose the topic.

The Humanist's creative factor is more mechanical than purely creative. While the Indigo Artist can pull a concept out of thin air, the Humanist is more comfortable replicating art or furthering a concept they have seen before. Their artistic skills are impressive, but seldom original. They themselves seem aware of this characteristic, often envying the pure artist. Their artistic talent does not carry over to their environment. Of all four types, they are the most disorganized and messy at home.

Barring genetic factors, they are usually thin and have healthy body shapes and sizes. They are curious about the human body and about emotional reactions. Stress is likely to take its toll on the human body for a Humanist in the eyes, ears, nose, throat, and legs. When this happens, a Humanist can reground himself by being with people he likes and by enjoying his music. The best of all worlds is to combine the two.

Humanists are the most active physically and can seem hyperactive at times. They also have very short attention spans. They are the most likely to be labeled ADD (Attention Deficit Disorder) or ADHD Attention Deficit Hyperactive Disorder). Nancy has often labeled the Indigos as floaters. Humanists are the prototype of this. As small children they wander around at night, float from activity to activity, and from one group of people to another. It is not that they cannot focus or settle. They simply assess a situation, process it faster than everyone else, determine if there is any point in engagement, and then move on.

Under stress, Humanists' bodies immediately go into motion in order to release the emotional process they are experiencing. When their self-esteem button is hit, they will get sick almost immediately. They have to act out their emotions. They don't know how not to behave this way. If left unchecked, their emotions can gain the upper hand. They can have fits of depression and will, occasionally, turn suicidal if not counseled. If they are withdrawn, the best method of dealing with them is to leave them alone for a few minutes and then to go to them and offer conversation.

Many Humanists are completely self-oriented. Their idea is the best. Their focus is on themselves all of the time. They lack the ability to gauge where others are coming from or what someone else might be feeling, except as it relates to them. They have difficulty seeing another's point of view. They must have the last word. This self-involvement hits them the hardest as a teenager and causes continual angst with parents and siblings. Eventually the Humanist can modify this behavior, but it takes a long time and patience on the part of others.

Humanists fear rejection. In relationships they are very sensitive and cannot tolerate being betrayed. Accepting others and being accepted by others is at the heart of their life purpose, so in their eyes, rejection is a basic denial of who they are. They do not have the ability to pass rejection off as "just an event" or "just this time." They do not analyze or rationalize as well as their fellow Indigo Conceptualist, who can more easily see the other person's point of view. To the Humanist rejection is about people, about being loved and accepted by their peer group and those they care about.

The negative side of the Humanist is the con artist, the one who manipulates others for the good of himself. The con artist steals the ideas of others, parading them as his own. He or she will talk his friends into wrongdoing. This can begin in early childhood -- copying a friend's homework or getting someone else in the group to do most of the work. In the workplace it looks the same. A negative Humanist always puts more thought and energy into figuring out how to get out of an action or how to gain from someone else's work than he does in the actual work itself. Male and female alike, negative Humanists are skilled manipulators, using their words and charm as weapons instead of personal assets.

Humanists have one more quality that comes as a mixed blessing. Of all the Indigos, they are the most naive. They are always the ones who get caught in any kind of mischief or wrongdoing. Wonderfully innocent, they will wonder what they did wrong when everyone else was "doing it" and then wonder why they were the only ones who got caught.

Current famous Indigo Humanists are Tiger Woods, Barak Obama, Princes William and Harry, and Michael Dell. Another Humanist, Mark Zukerberg, created Facebook, today's ultimate Humanist creation which globalizes and connects people around the world.

Humanists are the communicators, transmitting their thoughts and ideas through talking and writing from person to person. They are engaging, fun, casual, and social. They have had a busy first forty years, connecting everyone on the planet. Eventually they will spread the words, ideas, and philosophies of the other three Indigo types.

5

Artists – Animated Performers

*A*melia writes in her diary, "I had the WORST day EVER! I wanted to play soccer at school, but Joanie and Louisa didn't. They got the other girls to go on their side. I could see them trying to talk everyone into it. I told them that it would rain and they would get all wet. I just went inside and drew in my folder. But I could see out the window that they were playing anyway. They got their dresses wet. HAH! Louisa told me that it was fun to get wet. I was completely upset. I held it in and held it in, but when I got home I had to hurry to get my tear bottle out so I could put my tears in it. I cried and cried. It felt so good. I bet I have fourteen tears in it this time. I put the stopper in carefully so they will be protected."

Quintessentially Artist, Amelia illustrates the supersensitive and dramatic Indigo at her finest. Artists are the second most common Indigo after Humanists. Intensely creative, Artists are here to bring in new art forms in all areas, not just the fine arts. Their great gift and talent is to bring mankind the new artistic processes of the future. Their creations will become new classics. Their talents are remarkable, often manifesting themselves in full form while they are still children. They are the creators and artists of tomorrow.

Listen to the kind of music that appeals to them. They have unique hearing on another level that we cannot reach. They have an exaggerated sense of sound. They hear things the rest of us do not. Most of today's young people in the music world are Indigo Artists. They range from teenagers in garage bands to child prodigies who are already famous.

Music is their life. They may dance to it, sing or vocalize it, play it on their instruments, or draw while they listen to it. Indigo Artists create music using sound combinations, tempos, and rhythms not heard before. The rest of us can only listen and appreciate (or be horrified).

The ultimate performers, Artists are focused, dramatic, sensitive, and passionate. They radiate when they are performing. They pull their creative ideas out of thin air, effortlessly and endlessly. But this ability carries a price tag. The very creative and emotional nature that allows them to pull new designs and new art forms directly from the universe makes them more dreamy and fragile than the other Indigo types. Because they have received their "vision" from its source, they do not have the ability to see themselves as wrong. Their ego is their downfall. They are melodramatic and often unrealistic emotionally. They laugh and cry easily, parading their emotions for all to see. They can play victim easily, especially if their social standing is threatened.

Think of them as butterflies or orchids -- fragile and rare beauties. There are also days when they are peacocks, awing others with their sheer color and beauty but making a loud and raucous cry when disturbed. Artists are naturally graceful and always fastidious with their appearance. They are interested in whether they are pretty or not and whether things are going well. They want to find out whether they are happy or whether you are happy. They love the finer things of life, exhibiting a strong need for expensive and lovely things. They are never satisfied, always wanting more and more of whatever they have. While that may seem negative and impractical to others who share their daily life, that insatiable quality serves the Artist well because it keeps them embedded in their creativity and vision, seeking and wanting to bring more beauty to life.

Indigo Artists wear their beauty well. They love to wear the latest fashions and never pay attention to the price tag. When shopping, they will bypass the sale rack in favor of the highest quality. But they are also content to go home with no purchases at all if nothing meets their quality criteria. They love shoes! They are picky, picky, picky and usually do not like the choices anyone else makes for them. They are neat freaks; their closets are clean and organized. There is always plenty of room for the shoes. The Humanist can tolerate a mess; Artists are fastidious and meticulous. Others who live with or near Indigo Artists can tell you that they are high maintenance and dramatic.

As children, Indigo Artists should be directed toward the physical arts and crafts or any performing art. They can often try a dozen or more activities until they settle into one art form. They do not need to learn their talent; they intuit it. They only need discipline in the technique or art to perfect their form. Parents should introduce them to as many performing arts as possible. They need to have five or six processes in order to expand and develop their creativity and in order to get a sense of how their creativity feels to them individually. A wise parent should keep them motivated and focused on each discipline until the young Indigo gets bored, and then they should suggest another one. Quite frequently as teens or young adults, Artists will cross from one artistic endeavor to another. For example, there are several current ice skaters who excelled in gymnastics or even roller skating before they segued into ice skating. That multi-talented ability is common for the Indigo Artist.

At school, Artists are extremely bored by mundane reading, writing, and arithmetic. Ideally they perform more positively in a creative school for the arts or in an environment where they are allowed time every day for their talent. If the parents can't do that, then they should get to know Artist's teacher. If the teacher does not understand the Artist child's unique qualities, the child will not respect her, will not learn from her, and will make sure nobody else does either. Chapter 9 (Indigo Students, Indigo Teachers) deals with the classroom behavior of the Artists in more detail. They can be complex and difficult to handle in the classroom if their creativity is stifled. Their ego can also cause problems because they don't think they make mistakes. Frequently they are the ones whose body remains in the classroom but whose head goes home.

Who are Indigo Artists? Meet Jody, Louis, and Bao.

Jody lives in Australia. By day she is a primary teacher; at night she makes time for her passion, digital scrapbooking. A veritable Photoshop

Queen, Jody combines photos, words, and graphics into pieces of art that she uploads and posts on her favorite scrapbooking site for fellow hobbyists. Jody's hobby identity, "pagequeenjo," has fans all over the world, other moms who steal time from their day to turn pictures of their kids into artistic creations, preserving precious memories in a highly creative format.

Across the world another Indigo Artist, Louis lives in France. He is sixteen years old and attends school less than enthusiastically. Louis sees himself on stage playing his music to crowds everywhere. He plays guitar with a small group of friends, often composing their own music. He feels alive and purposeful when he is with his group, but he is unable to get the same kind of drive going elsewhere in his life. He uses his spending money to add to his music collection and is saving for a newer and better guitar.

In China, Bao is four years old. He lives far away from his family, new to his school. Bao was chosen for his gymnastic skills as a three-year old. He will receive elite training, excellent health care, and the possibility for many honors as long as his body can perform. Bao is adorable. He sparkles and is very capable of constant mischief. He loves gymnastics and already shows great promise.

These three Indigo Artists are talented, passionate about their art, and convinced that the world should share their enthusiasm. They spend long, long hours thinking about the next song, the next artistic design, or perfecting the current one. They are the designers of the future.

Indigo Artists have the same sense of entitlement that other Indigos have, but they exhibit it as performance. They think they are good, and they expect good treatment. They don't think they make mistakes. Their best quality is their drama because they refuse to be wrong. Capable of intense focus and long hours, Artists will work until they achieve perfection. They are willing to sacrifice their body sometimes for their art.

However, drama can be hard to live with occasionally. On the whole Artists like to get along with others and will do what is good for the whole. But unlike Humanists, Artists do not mind confrontation. They can become more and more dramatic in their presentation. In any kind of confrontational situation or argument, they will become more and more agitated and aggressive if the other person is not telling his or her truth. The Artist will push and push until they force others to get real with themselves. This can often be difficult for parents and people with other life colors who were socially trained to conform to polite conventions and to repress their hidden feelings.

In addition, Artists will perform in front of you, giving you the behavior you expect or require and then being sneaky behind your back. From their perspective, they are just being true to their truth. You are the one who is wrong. This can happen at home, at school, or in the workplace. When they begin to "zone out," know that inside themselves they have already decided they are right. You are just stupid. They withdraw to their creative side, preferring quiet detachment until they can be appreciated again.

At work, Indigo Artists are intensely creative and hard workers as long as the focus is on them or their art. If not, they will drop the activity and move to another endeavor where they can turn on their creativity again. What is important to an Artist in a job environment is to evaluate the place they will perform. To an actual performing Artist (singer, dancer, actor), the stage, lighting, and environment itself are important. It is critical that the Artist *look good* or present well. An Artist who is not front stage center still cares about an environment where he or she can perform correctly. Indigo Artists usually keep their area neat, picked up, and clean. Having a messy co-worker next door will irritate them.

Their body type can be thick or thin. Whichever, they do not have self-consciousness about it. They exhibit their stress in the head, shoulders, or neck. Like Humanists, when the Artists' self-esteem button gets hit, they will get sick almost immediately. Their therapy is their art and often their music. Like the Humanist, putting them together is the happiest of all combinations.

Negative Artists will either not put their work out for the world to see or will steal the art and concepts of others and claim it for their own. They can also draw or create violent, often visually graphic, art that is dark and disturbing. They can overdramatize situations until their opponents just relinquish their position and give up.

The Indigo Artist has one quality that no other Indigo type has and no other life color in Nancy's system as well. All Artists have some kind of fetish: shoe, finger, or foot. By fetish, we mean an inexplicably strong attachment to the object of choice. It develops in childhood, is not genetic or environmentally introduced, and defies logical analysis. The Artist does not question it nor consider it worthy of discussion by others. It simply *is*.

Famous Indigo Artists are easier to pick out than the other types. As mentioned at the end of Chapter 3, child prodigies like Jackie Evancho, the child with the amazing soprano voice is an Indigo Artist as is Akiane, the spiritual artist who began painting as a young girl. Most young people on the reality performance shows like *American Idol* or *So You Think You Can Dance* are Indigo Artists. Il Volo, the Italian operatic pop teen group (Piero Barone, Ignazio Boschetto, and Gianluca Ginoble) are all Indigo Artists. Artists are publishing books as children, having exhibits in galleries, and creating small businesses to sell software programs and video games which they designed themselves. Christopher Paolini, Indigo Artist / Humanist, wrote his first book *Eragon* as a teenager.

Indigo Artists have been the least quiet of the four types in their storm of influence, breaking the sound barriers of decency and appropriateness through their music. Indigo Artists in rap and hip hop music have affected millions of young people in every country of the world with blatancy of their music, lyrics, and violence. Marshall Brice Mathers III, otherwise known as Eminem, is an example of the genius of an Indigo Artist in this genre. He has spoken openly and frequently about his compulsive need to create poetry and music. Today music gives the reader a clear example of the constant turbulence, change, rebirth, and renewal of the Indigo storm and its aftermath as young Artists tear down established attitudes of the kinds of language and subject matter that can or should exist in lyrics and musicality. For those who are appalled, take heart. What is the very essence of music today will be completely different in five or ten more years. For those who find it exciting and freeing, it will still be different in five or ten more years as Indigo energy brings even further change.

Even in the technology world, creative design is an important factor. Sergey Brin and Larry Page, the co-creators of Google are both Indigo Artists. Another artistic genius in that field was Steve Jobs, a Violet with Indigo Artist aspects. These brilliant people used Indigo Artist qualities to bring new technological forms to the global audience.

There are countless young adult Indigos in the arts and entertainment field, especially in music. It serves no purpose to name or identify them further. The focus of this book is to concentrate on the Indigo energy and qualities, not just to tell who is and who is not an Indigo. What is important is to appreciate the talent and beauty they bring to our world today. What is also important to remember today is that Artists do not perform alone. Humanists talk about the Artist's talent, spreading their enthusiasm around the world and build the world-wide (and often very lucrative) audience for each Artist. Behind the scenes is the Conceptualist, building the stage, creating new sound and lighting systems, enhancing the visuals, and inventing the next level of equipment and technology for the Artist to use in his performance.

6

Conceptualists – The Think Tank

*C*onceptualist: I graduated from college and realized that I did not have *a job offer. I had applied to law school but had not yet received any acceptances. I didn't know what to do. So I walked over to the graduate school and signed up for a master's degree in public policy. Then I went home and wrote a computer program to help me decide what was the best option for me and to analyze the chances of my getting into law school. I had only applied to the top five. My grades were not top notch, although my LSAT score was nearly perfect.*

Humanist: Gee, Greg, at our apartment we make a pro and con list and then every-one talks it over. Then I decide what to do.

Artist: I just go to bed, have a good cry, and then when I wake up the next morning, I know what to do.

Conceptualist: You do what?

Center stage in the Indigo world is the Conceptualist, the genius behind the scenes who builds a new world via technology. Much less social than their Humanist friends and much less visible than the Artists, the Conceptualists show their enthusiasm for life in their projects and their work. Conceptualists view the future in terms of its technological possibility. They analyze the situation, lay out a plausible timeline, and then get to work and do it.

So far, there are fewer Indigo Conceptualists than Humanists or Artists because Humanists have to connect the world before the real work begins. This demographic is slowly beginning to change. Nancy feels that eventually Conceptualists will increase in number to nearly fifty percent of the population, more impersonal, more technical, and much more focused. Their work, their life, and their perspective will be more electronic.

Conceptual Indigos are project people. Their task is to introduce new concepts in technology, design, and mechanical processes. They are the ones who will draw new patterns and create new platforms for ways to work which the Humanists will use to bring about change. They like to take things apart and may or may not put them back together. They may become engineers, architects, project planners, and computer programmers and designers. Loners by nature, they are capable of long and hard hours of work on their project. They are brilliant with computers and with most forms of technology.

The Conceptualist Indigos, with their engineering mind, has little use for people who cannot work within the framework of their projects. There is no intended animosity on their part. It is more like, "you are either in or you are out." There is not room for a middle ground. On the job, Conceptualists will not tolerate intrusion. They want things in their time and in their way. They are the best at working from home because they can be in complete control of their work environment and can eliminate the social factor. When it is time for a break, they entertain themselves with a video game or reading a tech manual. They are totally into their current work - - focused and methodical. They are tomorrow's researchers, engineers, and scientists; they analyze the weaknesses and limitations of technology today and create the platforms of the future.

Since most Conceptualists are introverted, they do not care how others perceive them. They seldom appreciate the social aspects of work and often see them as intrusive on their time and focus. Their best skill at relating to other people is to analyze them because they are curious about how things function. Others may perceive them as devious; they see themselves as analytical. They do not tattle as children nor blow the whistle as adults. The Conceptualist will fire a subordinate or sabotage a peer until the other person gets thrown off the project. The Conceptual Indigo regards it as working for the ultimate good of the project and having control over all the factors to guarantee the highest quality. They do like to feel superior, both at home and at work.

A strong focus on analysis can often be a true asset. Conceptualists find it easier to get out of depression because they look for the source and then seek solutions. They will research means and methods of treatment to see if they can figure out how to resolve a situation they do not feel productive in.

Who are they in real life? Let's meet some.

Jake is a latchkey kid. At age eleven, he walks from his elementary school back home daily at 3:30 pm. Both parents do not arrive before 7:00, often bringing dinner home in a bag. Jake is perfectly happy with the situation. He likes the quiet time without his little sister. Jake finishes any homework he may have while he eats a snack. Then he moves to the activity he has looked forward to all day, his video games. Graphic and often violent, Jake likes the constant challenge, the speed, and the strategies he must use. Lately he has begun to think that some day he would like to create a game himself.

Seventeen hours time difference away, Ella and Adrian are graduate students at a prestigious university. Both are social science majors, and both are Conceptualist Indigos. They decided to go ahead and start their family before it was financially feasible because they realize that having a baby right in their home will give them non stop access to observe their very own infant, and later, toddler in action. They keep intensive video notes and spreadsheets of performance and behavior statistics, plotting them against norms. Ella and Adrian look at the situation as having a living science project for the next eighteen years right in the family room.

And finally, Eric, age sixteen, is a senior in high school. He speaks about his part time job. "I do tech support after school. I have to take calls from people who can't figure out the software, even though it isn't that hard. I hate the old ladies the most. The worst one was a woman who called in about getting started with the program. I told her to right click on the mouse and was about to give her the next direction, when she asked what a mouse was. I hung up. The phone rang again but I didn't answer it." There is nothing touchy-feely about the Conceptualist.

Physically, Conceptualists are larger in size than the Humanists or Artists. Their stress manifests itself through headaches, sinus problems, and in the back and legs. When the Conceptualists' self-esteem buttons are pushed, they will get angry and try to regain control of the situation. To alleviate stress, they need to get back to work on their project or in their game, an electronic situation they feel they can control. They are more stabilized in their body than Humanists or Artists and not usually hyperactive, although they can "ramp up" at times, wanting to do too many things with their project at once. Conceptualists do not radiate or sparkle.

They are the ones who love the order and structure of the military. They like the logical progression of a military organization where they can see a systematic and attainable means of superiority to strive for. Conceptualists are also the most militant, the ones who can transfer violence from their video games into actual life. Much less social than their Humanist peers, they do not dislike people, but people have to fit into their project or the Conceptual Indigo will just disregard them. People are their tools; if they can't use them, they will discard them, sometimes violently.

Conceptualist children are quiet and content to play alone. They can go to their room and entertain themselves for hours. They like intricate and inanimate toys, things they can take apart. They may or may not put them back together. Their ideal toys are Legos or blocks where they can design and build their own systems. Quite frequently, even putting them away involves storage systems and organizational structures that others may not realize. Conceptualist Indigos operate on a mental level, organizing, planning, designing, and analyzing. They are applied and industrious inside their head.

The Conceptual mind does not deal with pain -- only with "where is the boundary of existence?" They need to learn at an early age that all living things hurt when they are pushed beyond their capacity. The single most important thing a parent can teach them is that other people have feelings. They simply don't know this before they are two years old. Often just talking and explaining this to the toddler will be effective.

Conceptualists children are also addictive in nature. Parents of these children would do well to monitor their peers and work to keep their addictions healthy. Sports, martial arts, and religion provide healthy outlets for the Conceptual Indigo because they teach discipline, a sense of sportsmanship, and a feeling of belonging. All Indigos work for the good of the whole; Conceptualists are no exception, but they like to feel that they are the superior ones of the group.

Conceptual kids like war games and games with weapons. They are the ones who like the vicarious primal instincts of search and destroy that video games provide. They get the challenge, the intensity, the fight, and the kill -- all in the safety of their pajamas with a pizza in front of them. Inside their head, they are developing skills of logic, systems, structures, and patterns.

Negative Conceptualists will steal other peoples' work and claim it as their own. They are the hackers, either doing it themselves or teaching it to others to do for them. Negative Conceptualists will manipulate facts and statistics to meet their own ends. They are also the ones who make bombs and guns. Suicide bombers are nearly always Conceptualists or those trained by Conceptualists. All of the instances where children kill others occurs with Conceptualists. They think they are doing it to save the world. They are the ones who pull the trigger. Why? They are attracted to superiority and control, turning violent if necessary to win their game. If the game is in real life, so what?

If the Conceptualists were animals, what would they be? Think of the Big Cats, blending into the jungle or savannah. They spend most of their day, either drowsing or alert and waiting. Their patience, speed, strength, and cunning are extraordinary, a thing to be envied and also feared. They are the kings of their world, always in control, and always ready. When they strike, they go for the kill.

Sounds alarming, doesn't it? Will every Conceptualist exemplify this metaphor? Of course not. Most will quietly and efficiently add great benefit to the planet, designing new systems and technologies of tomorrow that we cannot even dream of today. However, nowhere has the perpetuation of the Indigo myth as "magical, special children" done more harm than to ignore this additional side of Indigo energy. Remember, they are here to show us tomorrow and all of its ramifications. If man is capable of great violence and evil, some Indigos will act that out in living color. The Conceptualists have the greatest potential for this.

7

Catalysts —The Visionaries

amon B. is a six-year old Hispanic male, unusually large for his age.
He is being raised by his grandparents in a large, Catholic family.
Ramon rarely speaks, has repetitive body gestures and occasionally
hurts himself, answers to few stimuli, and exhibits little response
to social cues. Ramon does like to paint and is capable of remarkably accurate
portrayals of animals and birds.

Bonnie lives in England near a medical center where she sees her doctors regu-
larly. She is twenty-two years old and has a rare genetic disorder that mandates
a quiet life filled with medical tests and treatment. Bonnie uses a computer to
describe her treatments in vivid detail. There are no contextual clues about her
reactions to either her disorder or her feelings about it.

Rarest and seldom observed, Indigo Catalysts are the least well adapted to human life. By definition, a catalyst is one who begins a change or event, especially without being involved in or changed by the consequences of that change. The Catalysts' task is to introduce new philosophies and religions. They will bring knowledge from consciousnesses not experienced on the earth plane before. They are the most rare of Indigo types, with only about 1 in 3,000. They can be as easy-going as Humanists but can fly into a rage in a moment. They are curious about everything, especially the human body and must experiment (sometimes on others) to observe the responses and limitations of the body. They can project an air of superiority to others who do not match the same mentality. Eventually they will begin to appear in greater numbers once old systems and structures are no longer in place and they can begin to bring in new theories and paradigms. Upon meeting one, the first thoughts from another would be to call them "extremists" or "eccentrics." They do not sparkle nor radiate good will or enthusiasm.

The Catalyst background is mental, not physical. They have an innate body of information that we do not have on this plane. They are quick-witted and very intelligent, quite often in the savant range. Their thoughts and ideas are very abstract, often seeming strange and inappropriate because they have gone over our heads completely.

Like the great blue whale, Catalysts have a thick, heavy body. Think of Orson Welles and Raymond Burr in their full maturity. They use this heavy body type in order to have greater latitude. They believe they have a "heavy task" so they select a body type that will protect them. Like the whale, they navigate through their world silently, infrequently relating to the vast seas around them. Beautiful in their own world, the rest of us have little sense of exactly what their world is or how it works.

The Indigo Catalysts exhibit their stress in the mouth, eyes, ears, nose, throat, and chest. They do not like the human body and frequently test its limits. They may exhibit strange and peculiar noises, simply trying to find out just what the human voice can do. What they actually do is try to find the boundaries of the human body through trial and error. They do not like being in the human body. Even as small babies, they do not like the fact that they cannot get the body to do what they want it to. Consequently, they sleep longer and more often than the other types. They need close supervision because they are high-risk children. They will expand our consciousness about what the human body can do. To date, many Indigo Catalysts have a genetic defect or serious health issue, even as a child. In this way they can see, test, and experience the limitations of the machine we call the body. It is part of their learning experience.

Normally just insensitive to others, they can also occasionally be cruel. When this happens, they feel that they are simply experimenting with the possibilities of human behavior. They do not understand the physical parameters of another person or another person's boundaries either. They do not have stored memories of pain, nor do they realize that they can create pain for someone else. They can easily stick their fingers into another person's eye or nose just to see what kind of reaction it will provoke. They mean no harm. It is a detached action, almost clinical in their observation process.

Catalysts benefit greatly from martial arts training as an opportunity to learn to funnel their energies, to ground themselves in their bodies, and to focus their thoughts from the abstract to the concrete. They need the introspective vision of inner control and outer contentment that these paradigms offer. Martial arts also teach the Indigo Catalysts how to release their frustration in a non-combative way. They are not content with the world the way it is now, but they cannot see the vision of the future just yet. Life here simply does not always make sense to them.

With siblings, the Catalyst can be withdrawn and remote, often causing difficulties. The Humanist can walk away from potential trouble, but the Conceptual and Catalyst will strike first and then walk away, becoming angry if the parent or authority figure punishes him or her. Parents need to learn to talk to everyone involved in the conflict and negotiate a successful resolution and understanding for all. It is necessary to have the patience and willingness to explain and re-explain social behavior to the Catalyst and to explain anti-social behavior to siblings of other types.

A good way to understand the Catalyst is to view him or her as a curious visitor to our planet. They are not personable, nor are they giving of themselves in any way. At best, they are field researchers, here gathering data. We do not have a concept of what their internal or mental spreadsheet looks like. Most people consider them weird.

All that said, however, they do exhibit some outstanding characteristics. They like the opportunity to be outside or in a physical activity, although a team sport can be bewildering to them. Water and nature are their therapy. At work they are completely focused on their project, paradigm, or philosophy, even to the exclusion of eating or other routines of daily life. They project an air of complete superiority.

They will become the great humanitarians of their generation, working for global causes. Their task is to work for the good and ultimate advancement of our planet. It is to fulfill the Indigo mission on earth. Those who are the most likely to adapt well here will work for the good of the whole, rather than just themselves. How can this happen if they are loners or often lacking in social skills? Certainly it will not be through a charismatic personality. But it is easy to envision a Catalyst publishing a research paper outlining a new world economic theory that the Humanists will put into use or to work with colleagues to isolate new genetic processes to eradicate diseases or to increase the human lifespan. Catalyst's intellectual gifts might be put to use in discovering and utilizing more ocean resources, thus providing cheaper sources for food or healing potential that can be distributed worldwide for pennies. Or perhaps tapping into the most mysterious of all -- space. It may be a Catalyst who provides the next step for colonizing other locations beyond our planet.

Many people who are identified with Asperger's Syndrome or with other mild forms of autism are Indigo Catalysts. It has been Nancy's observation of Catalysts with autism, that at least fifty percent of those diagnosed do not actually have autism. They simply absorb the cues from their environment and use them to their advantage. People leave them alone if they have a label like autism that says, "hands off." They do not know how to behave according to social rules; it is easier for them to withdraw. Their asocial behavior is a personal choice. Parents frequently buy into the autistic label because the child is quieter when he is left alone than forced into mainstream behavior. Our social norms today still insist that all people behave according to cultural "rules" about humans interacting with humans in socially acceptable ways. Today, most Catalysts are unable to do that, often preferring distance and solitude as their friends. We need to acknowledge their uniqueness and give them the necessary space for learning and growth that we cannot understand.

At school Catalysts are tough to deal with outside a special education classroom. They are typically class disrupters. They have no interest in history because their theories are for the future. They may have a narrow range of only one or two topics that intrigue them. They are not interested in what the teacher thinks they should learn. Of all the four Indigo types, they are the least likely to admit culpability or guilt. One possible strategy to focus their thinking is to introduce studies in marine biology or oceanography to them or concepts in space. They may or may not take to it, but they will appreciate the vastness.

Gene Roddenberry (1921-1991) was an American television producer, writer and futurist, a visionary whose Star Trek series took science fiction audiences "where no man has gone before." Roddenberry broke social barriers of race and gender equality in his futuristic plot lines. He envisioned a world that had conquered hunger, disease, and other social problems on earth and had moved into the dimensions of space and time travel. He envisioned a world that Catalysts will help bring into actuality.

Raising Indigo Children, Being Indigo Parents

he following is a personal account from a Yellow (life color) father about his Indigo child, age six. "We had just moved into our brand new house, after a stressful six months waiting for it to be built. It was late February, still fairly chilly outside. At dinner one night, my wife was tired and bitchy after a day of unpacking and trying to get our two girls to finish fixing up their rooms. She started in on a tirade that threatened to disrupt the entire dinner, thus ending an already stressful day on a negative note. I thought I'd pitch in and do the firm parent thing. I looked at both girls sternly and said, 'I've had enough. If you want to live with boxes, move into the garage. There are plenty of them out there.' Our Indigo daughter left the table after hurrying through dinner. The other daughter sat silently at the table on the verge of tears through the whole meal. All of a sudden the Indigo appeared, her arms filled with stuffed animals, pajamas, a pillow, and two pair of underwear. 'Fine,' she stormed. 'You want me to live in the garage; I'll move to the garage.' She slammed the door shut and began arranging boxes in her new living space. My wife looked at me and said, 'Good job. What are you going to do now?' Today we all look fondly on that incident as the 'idiot father' episode. I learned a valuable lesson, never to threaten my children with something I could not back up."

There is no doubt about it, parenting is hard work. This has been true in every age since time began. Parenting begins with hormonal changes to the prospective mother and splashes over to the father. It most certainly starts actively the day an infant comes home. Parenting does not stop at age sixteen or eighteen; in fact, it never stops. We are not born knowing how to be good parents, nor do any of us make effective decisions every day. Some people get reasonably good parents to use as role models; others do not. These certainties rang true throughout the ages and are still true with Indigo children. There are some additional areas, however, where parenting Indigos requires a different set of guidelines.

In many ways, it is necessary to rethink our definition of parenting in order to provide the best environment for Indigo children. Adults assume that *shaping* our children is the exact nature of what a parent should do. Most good parenting begins with meeting the child's basic needs of food, clothing, and shelter, followed equally with protection and safety. Parents then go on to impose moral and religious values, character and social training, and contextual values for the larger world. Individual families add attitudes, prejudices, outside interests like sports or hobbies, and occasional inputs of formal knowledge in subjects of interest to the family. Most often, the authority structure is such that parents *provide* all of the above and children *absorb* them, preferably in an undiluted form. This is where the breakdown occurs with the Indigo. They just are not into direct absorption when their internal values may contain different information.

As far as parents are concerned, Indigo children have four basic needs: lots of love, a benevolent structure, conscious guidance, and the opportunity to display their uniqueness. Indigo children themselves believe they have four needs too: junk food, a cell phone and other media devices, freedom to make choices by themselves, and someone who understands them, i.e. their peer group. They consider their parents to be taller people who help them reach things until they can reach for themselves.

In actuality, that is not too far from the truth. Parents should guide -- not teach. They should help and assist Indigos to do things they cannot yet do -- reach up as they grow. Young Indigo children feel that they have to do things their way. After age sixteen, they assume the right to do things their way *all the time*. Guiding them allows for exposure to different beliefs and the opportunity for children to formulate their own opinions as they grow. This is certainly contrary to the way most homes and families operate. It is important to recognize and then remember that Indigos bring their own plan. Most rebellions at home occur when the Indigo's inherent internal wisdom or need for experimentation with other forms of thinking clashes with the parents' environmental training and authority structure.

All Indigos do love home and roots. They are strongly influenced by what goes on at home -- either positively or negatively. One interesting dynamic to observe is that the Indigo child will play out the mother's emotions. If mother is moody, the Indigo child will be moody. If mother is happy and content, the child will be the same. The Indigo child will always pay more attention to mother than to father, but the Indigo will be more objective with their feelings about their father.

Today's Indigo children are flexible and can carry their relaxed approach to life into split households. If parents divorce, they can adjust to splitting their time with both parents. They are willing to adapt to Dad's way when they are with Dad, and Mom's way when they are with Mom. Most of the time, they are also willing to carry messages back and forth, sometimes unintentionally. However, those who go with their dad when they are too young will self-destruct.

Indigos love to be right in the skin of whomever they are with. And conversely, they can get under one's skin faster than anyone. As illustrated in the vignette at the beginning of the chapter, dealing with them directly never seems to go quite the way one plans. Indigo children seem to be able to outthink and outwit their parents and teachers at an amazingly early age. They also have a sense "street smarts" that gives them an uncanny awareness of how things work socially.

Not only can Indigos outwit their parents, but they can also outmaneuver them as well. Indigos make storms in their own homes, sometimes a minor squall, and sometimes a full-blown hurricane. Today's news stories are full of incidents reporting youngsters legally divorcing their parents or of calling the police or having their parents arrested for drug abuse or breaking other laws. In fact, when pushed too far, the Indigo Conceptualist will carry his or her anger to the farthest extreme.

These behaviors are happening globally. A good read is *Nujood, Age 10 and Divorced*, by Nujood Ali, an Indigo Artist. Nujood was a female child in Yemen, who, according to tradition, was married to a thirty year old man who abused her daily. Nujood broke centuries of silence from this custom by divorcing him in open court and then by publishing her story for a worldwide audience in hopes that other young women in oppressed countries would take heart from her story. Books and other published accounts of young females breaking with tradition are appearing around the world. Indigos will simply not keep silent about parental injustices as has been the habit for so long. They are using their most effective and consistent tool, technology and the media, to make themselves heard.

There is no magic in effective parenting. It requires consistent, hard work. Proven strategies that work with Indigo children also work with other life colors. And strategies that work with one type of Indigo may not be as effective with other types. But here is the bottom line for parenting an Indigo. Be open and honest. Tell them the truth, and expect to be told the truth in return. Know your child, and know what messages and signals he or she sends. Respect them as individuals and expect respect in return. Play fair. Know that if you play games, they will play games right back. Love them, and you will be loved back. Indigo children who are talking to you and keeping an open line of communication are less a cause for concern than the ones who give you no idea who their friends are, what they do on the computer, or what they are thinking.

What are some techniques for dealing with them? Learn the art of bribery and negotiation. Find out what they love and bargain with it. If it is the computer or a video game, let them earn time with that activity. If it is playing dress-up or having a video, let them earn the time to do it. Indigos understand the clarity of negotiating and respect the fairness of the process. While we have been trained to think bribery is a negative parenting choice, the Indigo does not see it in this way. They regard it as business -- as long as there is equity and fairness to both sides.

Another effective strategy is to use technology in every way possible. Use it as entertainment, information seeking, negotiation for chore accomplishment, and with teens, use it to keep the communication channels open. Play video games together. Watch media together. Parents, watch your child's reactions to what they see through the media. Learn about young people today by watching them on television and in movies. And, at some point, recognize that your children will know more and be able to do more with technology than you ever will. Let them teach you what they know. Finally, one caveat. Parents must also closely monitor what their children are doing on the computer. Use the parent safety programs that are in place to prevent your children from wandering into (or seeking out) sites that are age and content inappropriate.

Indigo children are uninhibited, free, open, and honest about themselves. Parents should know that Indigo siblings have relationship dynamics just like anyone else. They do not hide their emotions. Humanists and Artists get along well most of the time until the Artist is into his or her art. If the Humanist just wants to talk and play, the Artist will get upset and dramatize his or her distress. If the Humanist is seeking an opportunity to tease or needle the Artist, the situation will escalate rapidly. The Humanist and the Conceptualist will always have problems when they are together. Conceptualists have control issues and will frequently try to exhort some form of physical control over the Humanist. Parents need to be aware of these dynamics in order to work with their children to avoid on-going problems. They also need to instill positive communication and problem solving strategies. Humanists respond best to talking things out; Artists need to feel that they are right from their point of view, and the Conceptualist needs to feel he has won. Does that sound tricky? Yes, but the wise parent will keep working the situation until each child feels his point of view has been voiced and respected.

Indigo children do not like to sleep alone. Many of them are "night crawlers," wandering from bed to bed at night, hoping the parents will take them in. Occasionally a sibling or the family dog will do just as well. Depending on the parenting style, this works well in some homes and can cause problems in others.

Indigo children need to be in preschool by the time they are three because they are very curious and ready to experience a larger world than is provided at home. By age three they will do what five year olds used to do. It is important to find their boundaries and work within them. Humanists especially need the social context of playing with many children that home schooling does not allow for unless the home school environment allows for play groups, church or neighborhood mixed group sessions, or occasional large group social activities.

Indigos need toys with built in ingenuity and complexity. This helps keep their attention focused and develops their thinking skills early so they are ready for computers when the time comes. Computer use is often sequential and cumulative; Indigo children need to start developing these skills early. Additionally, complex toys provide the intellectual challenge that the Conceptualist needs. Many toys are so lacking in depth or complexity of thought that the Indigo will soon wander off to the next activity, adding fuel to an observer's opinion that the child is hyperactive. Perhaps his or her mind is just understimulated.

To be certain, some parents are against putting their children into games and technology that open doors to material that is too old for them, to addictive behaviors, or simply to a prolonged lack of human interaction or physical exercise. Maintaining balance is the key. Parents must be vigilant to ensure that their children have adequate time daily for other types of entertainment, outdoor play, social interaction with other children, and time with family. It is all too tempting to let the computer or gaming device become babysitter, just as television did in previous decades. Nevertheless, Indigos are here to expand human potential through technology. Those children who do not have early exposure to technology and its vast universe of potential will be left in the dust.

Humanists are the most easy-going of all children to have. Good-natured and enthusiastic, they expect every day to be fun and interesting. They literally play out the game of living right before your eyes. Since they are the world's globalizers, they know more about people than anyone else, demonstrating innate people skills early in life. Natural born teasers, Humanists will always hit your funny bone.

The flip side of their skill with human nature, though, is that they also can spot your vulnerability from a long way off. Humanists will push parents' buttons easily and quickly. As long as you don't push them, they will stay cooperative. If you push your Indigo child back, however, he or she will show you how truly nasty a person can be. Tempers on both sides will ignite and move from a slow burn to raging fire.

Moms and dads of Humanist children may notice that they do not take naps or sleep as easily as other children. Humanists are into fun, games, and people. They want to know what makes people tick. They fear that if they go to sleep, they will miss something. These children also talk incessantly, and they do not talk unless they know someone is listening. They can jabber away in the back seat of a car, secure in the knowledge that whoever is driving hears them and will respond appropriately. Humanists like television shows with people their age, even as toddlers, absorbing human interactions and behavior from what they watch.

Parenting an Indigo Artist is a delight. They sparkle, entertain, and perform at the drop of a hat. Most Artists display their talents early. A wise parent has only to provide materials for them to create with -- plenty of dress up clothes, a stage, art supplies, an inexpensive musical instrument, or the opportunity to take a sampling of lessons. As mentioned in the chapter on Artists, these children have multiple gifts and "grow their creativity" in more than one area at a time. Parents must be patient as they move from one type of creativity to another. Most Artists will narrow the field eventually, but some will choose to remain multi-dimensional with their gifts.

As children and teens, Artists are probably the moodiest of all Indigos and the most devious. They think they are right in everything they do. Therefore, disputes with parents are inevitable. There are days when parents of teenage Artists can feel like they are on a roller coaster, moving from dramatic highs to moody blues at the drop of a hat. The best single management strategy for the Artist child is to get him back into his creativity until you have time to talk and sort things out together. Psycho-drama works especially well with Indigo Artists. They love the role playing and the entertainment factor involved.

Parents of an Artist can usually use the fifty percent guideline when experiencing one of their dramatic events. Fifty percent of the story they are acting out is probably true (to the Artist.) The other fifty percent is their over-dramatization. While it is important to give the Artist the stage, or in other words, listen to their story, after awhile, the wise parent will also work to bring the Artist back to a calmer perspective and perhaps the realization that the other participants in the drama had their own point of view as well.

Conceptualist children are much quieter than their Humanist brothers or sisters. They prefer structured toys and games but will smash or destroy them if they get frustrated. Parents often appreciate the Conceptualist child because he can play by himself for long periods of time, providing his own interior babysitter. These highly intelligent children will show a great aptitude for computers and computer games, especially those that have strategy and complexity. These children are not into as much conversation and human interaction as the Humanists or Artists are. A wise parent will approach the Conceptualist by asking to spend time with him in his project. "Can we build it together?" "Can I play the game too," taking care not to disturb the over-all system the child has established.

One of the single most important things that parents or grandparents of Indigo Conceptualists can do for the child is to help him or her with communication and social skills. The Conceptualist is weakest in this area. They do not understand their own feelings so they lack the ability to communicate them to others. They also have no concept of social nuances or behaviors with others. Parents need to model, discuss, and reinforce positive examples of good social skills for these children. It is not that they are incapable of learning; it is just that Conceptualists do not intuit social behavior like their Humanist brothers or sisters, and they do not know how to compute or articulate their own feelings.

Difficulty parenting the Conceptualist begins with the child's need to be superior and in control of whatever activity he is in. When difficulties arise, a wise parent can also balance him or her out with sports or martial arts or move him back into his hobby, game or project, again, until there is a chance for clear and honest communication.

As mentioned in Chapter 7, Nancy has seen and observed the patterns of the fewest Catalyst children because there are not very many as of yet. Because Catalysts have demonstrated the slowest adaptation to living here, it appears that parents of these children have their work cut out for them. Many Catalysts have health problems or fall somewhere in the autism syndrome. Others just do not want to communicate. They are unaware of their feelings and spend much of their time just trying to get used to the human body. However, their talents are prodigious. Their interests are global and humanitarian. They have innate wisdom and knowledge that cannot be accounted for. They may demonstrate interest in philanthropic causes at a very early age. Or they may choose a focus of interest and research far beyond their years, preferring to do little else but immerse themselves in their interest or cause.

Working with Catalyst children provides the greatest challenge for parents because the best strategies do not necessarily work with them. As mentioned before, Nancy has observed that many Catalysts so far have been diagnosed with autism. She is convinced that autism is environmental. As an aside, she has never seen evidence that autism is related to immunizations. In addition, it is her observation that many of those diagnosed do not fit the color vibrations she associates with autism. Nevertheless, her advice is the same for parents of children who exhibit behaviors consistent with autism: work with the experts both in diagnosis and in treatment. Nancy believes that the Humanists who are placed on the autism syndrome will respond best to standard treatments and behavior modifications for autism. The Catalysts may not benefit from these treatments because they like being left alone. Catalysts can benefit from some form of martial arts, disciplines which channel their energy and focus if they are willing or able to engage in those disciplines. Water and water activities also calm Catalyst children.

With all four types of Indigo children, parents need to realize that communication is the key. Parenting is not the place for "don't ask; don't tell" mentality. Those parents who can communicate openly with their Indigo are those parents who are preparing their children for the future. Indigos work well with rational explanations and fair choices. They do not work well with the adult rule, i.e. "I'm the adult, therefore, I make the rules," especially if those rules are arbitrary or irrational. Talk to them as if they were an adult. If you sit and explain things to them, they will absolutely comply with your wishes if they are reasonable. If they say no, say "how would you handle it to suit me?" or "These are the results I need. How are you willing to work with me?" Parents who try these questions will be surprised at the positive responses they can get from their children.

As illustrated in the vignette at the beginning of this chapter, disciplining an Indigo is not always easy. The days of "because I said so" are gone. Both Artists and Humanists are extremely sensitive; if they are given punishment without explanation, they can develop problems. If parents threaten their Indigo, the child will make them follow through. And if a parent promises an Indigo something, he or she had better stand good on the promise. It is also best never to forbid them. Instead explain why their idea has negative consequences and then make a decision about moving forward together. Forbidden fruit has twice the allure.

Another technique is to provide Indigos with choices so they are the ones who make their own decisions. The Indigo life color comes with its own inherent sense of what is right for them. These children have their own answers and rebel when someone else tries to override their choice. Yes, that challenges our understanding of the basic and predominant role of parents. But the key is to offer the Indigo a variety of choices and then "load" the choices so that the Indigo makes the one the parent wants him or her to make. Indigos are open to doing things they do not like if presented with logical and fair explanations. They are also open to negotiating if the parent or teacher offers them something they consider valuable. Indigos like to feel that they have a vote, even if their choice does not result in the final outcome.

Indigos do not feel guilt imposed on them by others (including mother or father.) They may impose guilt on themselves if they feel they have not lived up to their own potential. When an Indigo throws a tantrum, he or she is experiencing a time of great sensitivity. The tantrum, however, is very controlled; once the parent gives in, the Indigo will stop the behavior immediately. The tantrum, then, is really more of a performance than out-of-control behavior. Indigos also can show perfect timing with their tantrums. They will wait until the parent is the most vulnerable before they begin to act out. The more dysfunctional the parent, the more flippant the Indigo will behave.

The only time Indigo children truly lose control is when things are too busy or frenetic and they become physically exhausted. When Indigo children become unusually quiet, then the parent needs to start talking with them. When Indigos are in the doldrums or move to a passive state, then they are in a time of indifference. Children under this kind of extreme stress can become non-functional. It is critical to not let them stay this way as it can lead to a lifetime of emotional scar tissue. It is more important to be functional than correct. Parents should do all they can to allow extra latitude with this Indigo and to seek out whatever is necessary to move the child back into a functional life. Later they can resort to therapy or the type of strategies that usually work with this child.

When the Indigos' self-esteem button gets hit, they get sick almost immediately. Quiet, reclusive behavior means they are stressed. The parents' task is to manage them carefully while they are stressed and to try not to stifle their natural exuberance and enthusiasm. In the best of worlds, Indigos do well as youngsters from six to ten years of age when they are given the opportunity for periodic, independent counseling from a professional. This experience can give the Indigo an objective forum to express his fears and is an excellent preventive approach to avoid major outbursts of anger.

Nancy also recommends finding one or more creative processes for all Indigo children as a place to put their excess energies. Certainly, some seem to benefit from medication in order to adjust to the slower pace that still exists in today's world. However, she strongly advises exploring all other possible options before subjecting them to medication which alters their energy level.

Indigo teenagers are the same as teenagers in every generation, only perhaps more exaggerated. They are rebellious, independent, and driven to break every rule authority imposes. For centuries teens have used drugs, consumed alcohol indiscriminately, and experimented with sex before body and mind had had a chance to work together. These behaviors are certainly not exclusive to Indigos. However, in the past teens did not do them in the percentages that occur today. Most Indigos are willing to break every parental barrier long before they are sixteen or eighteen.

The strategies for dealing with them are the same as dealing with Indigo children of other ages. Talk to them. Keep the door open to a successful line of communication. Try not to dictate to them; rather ask their opinion. Let them have a voice. Negotiate with them when possible. Offer them options, and guide them toward the healthiest choice. Most of all, let it be known that you are willing to work together.

As if the teen years are not difficult enough, Nancy has also observed that Indigos are not quick to leave home. They like casual living arrangements but do not love dorm life. If they complete college away from home, they are likely to move back home during their early 20's or to find friends to form a sense of "family" in apartment living. Scientists predict that it will not be unusual for young people today to live to be 100 years or older. It is unrealistic to expect them to know what they want to do for the rest of their life in their early twenties. This is a generation who has watched both parents work hard, sometimes each holding two jobs as the economy has fluctuated. Part of their reluctance to get out into the world may be due to fact that they are not eager to face these difficulties themselves. Today's young adult Indigos see their parents struggle to stay afloat financially, struggle to stay in or leave a marriage where they were unhappy, and struggle to find happiness in a changing world. Many do not view the adult world as a positive place to be. In addition, many Indigos still have not gotten clear with themselves about where they are headed. They are just not quite ready to meet the world head on.

Most of the early Indigos are now parents themselves. Their parenting characteristics are entirely consistent with their basic nature -- casual, relaxed, easy-going, and perfectly willing to break traditional rules of parenting. Indigos themselves make good parents, sharing the burden and responsibilities equally. Not only is this natural to them, but it is also the wish of their Indigo children. Indigos also make good parents because they will talk straight to their children, and their children will talk back to them even straighter.

It is fun today to watch Indigo parents in public. They wear their love for parenting and for their children proudly. Take a stroll through the local zoo or airport. Someone wearing a Baby on Board t-shirt may well be the father carrying his infant in the baby carrier while mom totes the luggage. Indigo parents divide the child-rearing tasks much more evenly than in previous generations just like they do with housekeeping. Most are willing to swap time and tasks to get the job done efficiently.

It is also worthy of note, however, that most Indigo children today around the world are raised by a village. Even in industrialized countries, almost all mothers work. Consequently children are placed in daycare as early as six weeks old. Looking at the situation objectively, it is clear that most Indigo "siblings" are children in their daycare setting who spend by far more hours a day with them than their actual sisters or brothers. This is the new norm, a widening of the family concept and an early indication of why globalization is happening so easily. Most urban day-care facilities have a mix of many ethnicities, languages, and beliefs. All are welcome.

As recommended in other chapters, Nancy advises the reader to watch today's television shows to step into Indigo mentality regarding family life and parenting. Many viewers from an older generation regard today's shows as a wide array of dysfunctional families and mayhem home management. Other viewers see the cultural breakdowns for what they are: new beliefs about who makes good parents, the continual struggle to keep all family members up to the pace of modern living, and love that is not just about providership or a static family structure.

Technology has provided instant help and innovation to family life. "Nanny cams" have allowed anxious parents to view their child's safety with a babysitter or caregiver. Young children are connected to grandparents and other relatives who live far away via social media, cell phones, and the ability to share photos and videos with loved ones as soon as they are taken. Parents have access to more immediate feedback from medical test results on their children or grade reports from the child's teacher. Neither time nor distance prevents parents or other family members from being connected to their children and their lives. Perhaps best of all, there is a wealth of information about parenting and parenting skills available on the Internet. No parent can claim ignorance today regarding good parenting practices with so much information available.

But, as with all things, there is a frightening side to the use or misuse of technology related to parenting young children today. A high school teacher relates an incident that happened recently in her class. "I do not usually have a problem with cell phone use in class. Students know that once the bell rings, they must put them away. But last week I was checking roll and noticed that Cora had her cell phone on her desk. The top was flipped open. I walked quietly over to her desk and said, 'Cora, you know you need to put the phone away.' She replied, 'Please don't make me, Mrs. Fonseca. I'm babysitting.' 'What?' I asked incredulously. Cora went on to explain that her mom could not miss any more days of work or she would lose her job. Mom put the web camera on the laptop at home in the family room, focused on Cora's little sister, who listlessly watched television from the sofa. Cora told me that she had to keep an eye on the sister until she finished school or let her mom know if something unusual or frightening happened." Cora had to be at school for only three periods, and then she was leaving campus to go back home for the rest of the day. Neither Cora nor her mother thought it was the best solution, but both felt boxed in by their academic or work circumstances. The little sister was home alone, sick, and with no adult on the premises.

An even more dramatic Webcam incident happened with an Indigo mother and her first baby, an infant only three months old. We'll call the Mom Brittany and the baby Jacob. Brittany was frequently overwhelmed with both the time and energy commitments of having a new baby. One morning she called her own mother in another state, and in a state of near panic, said, "Mom, I really need your help! I am going crazy. Can you sit on your computer for an hour and watch Jacob while he sleeps? I have got to get out of the apartment and take a run. It will only be an hour. He just fell asleep and always sleeps well at this time of day. Please, Mom, help me. I'll only be gone an hour." Brittany left the apartment before her mother had a chance to respond. Infant Jacob slept quietly for one hour while his grandmother in another state watched helplessly, furious at being placed in a situation where she had no control. How can this happen? Because technology today allows the possibility. When entitlement meets technology, potentially dangerous incidents can and will occur.

There are no fairy tales about good parenting. Rapunzel and Cinderella had to pay their dues before they could find the Prince and Live Happily Ever After. Rapunzel's mother was forced to give her up, and Rapunzel was eventually locked away in a tower. Cinderella lost her mother, and her benevolent but weak father gave her over to the wicked stepmother. Hansel and Gretel's father abandoned his children. Romulus and Remus had it even worse. Little Red Riding Hood had to navigate an unfriendly forest to take food to her impoverished grandmother, only to find Grandma victimized by a predator. It appears that our archetypal mythology does not promise much in the way of guidelines for parenting or hopes for an easy childhood.

In other cultures rite of passage customs and literature show an introduction to puberty and the adult world as isolation from the tribe and then the necessity to overcome a difficult task alone. In many cultures today children still undergo some kind of physical mutilation as part of the process to adulthood. Even Harry Potter wore a scar right from the start.

Clearly childhood is not for sissies, and good parenting skills are not cultural expectations. Indigos will change this. Indigo Humanists will rewrite the history of parenting through the basic behaviors they already exhibit: through parenting and raising children as a partnership, through communicating clearly and honestly, through accepting and honoring who their children are versus forcing them to become a predefined image, and finally, through a qualitative kind of loving that does not acknowledge barriers nor understand separateness.

9

Indigo Students, Indigo Teachers

My Journal (Grade 2)

Mr. Gonzalez said to write what we did yesterday. I saw Mrs Strom teaching multi-plication to Tim and Jose in after care. I looked at it and decided to learn it. I learned it. Grandpa made me show him when I got home. He was surprised I new it. He gave me some problems. I figurd them out. I also saw a book at the back of our room on cursive. It looks fun. If Mr. Gonzalez will copy some pages, I will learn it myself.

The Indigo quiet storm is nowhere more evident than in their performance and behavior in today's schools. As we wrote in the opening chapter of this book, "A storm is a confluence of unstable energy moving about in the atmosphere to bring about change. On earth, storms occur as part of nature; man can neither halt nor prevent them. Man can only wait them out and then determine a course of action, either using his resources to adjust and adapt to new circumstances or to behave as a hapless victim. In the aftermath of a storm, rebirth and renewal can occur." The Indigo academic storm is happening now in several significant ways.

The destructive aspect looks bleak. Students are dropping out of school in increasing numbers, especially in urban areas. This is a global trend, not a national one. The traditional education system is broken, despite the billions of dollars spent on it every year. Curriculum, textbooks, and testing have become politicized and stagnant. Traditional school building design cannot provide the modifications necessary for technological advances. Inside the classroom, children are bored, unmotivated, and restless. Yesterday's industrialized system of churning out students in an assembly line progression worked for several hundred years. Today's system seems to be imploding rapidly, and we cannot quite see the education of tomorrow.

What do the Indigos have to do with this? In Chapter 3 we discussed the fact that Indigo energy is androgynous (both masculine and feminine combined). Boys are becoming more feminine in their drive, energy, and purpose, and girls are becoming more masculine in their drive, energy, and purpose. We can see this in rapid shifts in student populations. Increasing numbers of boys are dropping out of education, beginning in high school. They are unmotivated and unwilling to pursue a road that (for them) looks like it is going nowhere. At the same time, current population statistics show higher female enrollment in college, medical, dental, and law schools. More girls are becoming engineers, scientists, and business executives. Yes, in part, these changes are a reflection of the failure of educators to meet boys' learning needs. But in larger part, it is also indicative of the re-shifting of Indigo energy patterns. To give greater appeal to boys in school, curricula and student work needs to be less a recitation of facts and more an opportunity to create. Most Indigos are very creative. They require guidance in their curiosity rather than explicit instruction or dogma delivered by rote. Worksheets bore them because they do not allow for creativity, thinking, or the type of interaction and involvement they receive in their video games.

Could education be better? Of course. There has been much hypothesis about how Indigo children need to be taught. Nancy Tappe said forty years ago that the Indigo child would benefit psychologically with schooling that was more individualized to meet their needs. She also added at the time that all students, regardless of labels, would learn more successfully from education processes that are student-centered and that allow for more self-paced learning. This is true and has always been true for all children in all times. But private education is neither reality nor practicality on a global basis. All Indigo children do not require private education in order to learn successfully.

The fact is that Indigo children are in school in nearly every part of the world every day. Most are with dedicated teachers who are doing their best with the materials they have to teach them the rudiments of reading, writing, math, and some form of science and social science. In addition, most children have access to more creative subjects as well. In the most remote places on earth -- small villages in India, distant areas of Mongolia, and remote regions of Africa and South America, children have seen and used computers, cell phones, and televisions. They have found and accessed information through Google or YouTube. Some young children are using proactive methods to educate themselves when they wish to move faster through a subject or simply learn something besides what is going on in the classroom. Even in the worst schools in urban cities, some children learn productively every day and graduate their school to the next successful step of their lives.

However, education can do much better. In order to reflect Indigo energies, education also needs to be much faster. Today's generation of children, most of whom are Indigo, grew up from infancy watching images and getting their input from television and video games. Some parents placed their children in front of Mozart for Babies, expecting them to start brain development immediately (with a naive assumption that their brains were not already developing.) Other parents used the TV as a babysitter, entertainer, and early educator. Children were kept busy and quiet for hours with media input. Kindergarten educators to-day give credit to *Sesame Street* and the broad range of programming for young children for teaching kids most of the pre-reading skills they have in place before they begin elementary school. By the time a toddler is eighteen months old, he or she knows how to insert a DVD care-fully into the player and how to push a button in the right place on the remote control to begin a movie. They are media skilled even before much speech begins. Today's children know how to absorb and interpret multiple, rapid visual and auditory images per second; that is their norm.

But the downside is also immediately evident. By the time children reach grades one, two, or three, their school day consists of reading black words on white paper in outdated texts and in completing black line work-sheets on white paper. Little surprise then that students are bored in a classroom focused on worksheets or long reading passages or pages and pages of math problems with only occasional media input as a reward.

Their homework has no visual nor auditory context beyond a paper product. Indigo kids in school are bored! They are under-stimulated, and their learning needs are under-addressed. Consequently, they tune out their teachers and can't wait to get back home to television or their game device. Plato said, "Through education we need to help students find pleasure in what they have to learn." That was twenty-five hundred years ago. Nowhere is that thought more necessary than with children today. For students to find pleasure in education today, curriculum creators must utilize technology, media, games, and other processes with rapid enough visual and auditory input to keep their minds engaged.

However, one cannot blame Indigos for the creation of the computer, video games, or television nor for their resultant addictions to them. In Nancy's color system, Violets were the creative force behind television and video games. The Indigos are just here to show mankind the implications and use of these devices -- both good and bad. There is never one single cause and effect for an isolated identification group. Violets influenced and affected the advent and adjustment of Indigos, just as Indigos will influence and affect the group that comes after them. Indigos in school are fast-forwarding education's need to change via their increasing drop-out rates and indifference to outdated and outmoded teaching models.

All Indigo children are not ADD (Attention Deficit Disorder) or ADHD (Attention Deficit Hyperactive Disorder). Many do seem to resonate at a higher energy than other colors. Time is speeding up, and what seems too fast for us is just right for the Indigos. In addition, there are other factors that can add to the fact that today's children seem so much hyperactive than previous generations. Another factor that Nancy noticed when Indigos started coming in was that they have a larger liver than previous colors. This assists them indirectly to absorb and utilize the huge amounts of junk and processed foods available today. Foods are much more highly processed and have many more additives than they did in all other eras. This is amplified by the fact that children today get much less outdoor play or exercise than generations before them, especially those children not actively engaged in a sport. These cultural changes in diet and exercise also contribute to the high-energy patterns of many Indigo children.

There is no doubt that many children in today's classroom are multi-focused, whether they are labeled with some kind of deficiency or not. They pay attention to many things at once. Many are hypersensitive to the stimuli around them. At home their attention is also multi-focused. They multi-task. They do homework with friends, to music, over chat rooms, with TV on, and playing a game -- all simultaneously. Today, in their communication factor, email is too slow. Twitter, texting, and faster communication forms are predominating. Indigos want instant information and instant results. They want the freedom to be able to move on to the next activity instantly.

Most experienced educators know that children's needs in the classroom have changed dramatically in the last 20 years. Indigo learners are creative, often hyperactive, and easily bored. They heartily dislike inconsistency; therefore, computers make the best teachers for them, with teachers there for personalized help when needed. Indigos are technological geniuses and have no inhibitions when interacting with computers or new technology. They excel in classrooms where there are a variety of activities, and they have free choice of rotation among them. Options allow them to float from activity to activity according to their internal pacing. No doubt about it, this is not the kind of education structure that has been in place around the world for centuries. *In several basic areas then, teaching Indigo children calls for a complete reversal of thinking from traditional education.*

The first change is obvious and has already begun. Integrating technology into the classroom is a given. If Indigo children have come to globalize humanity through technology, then technology is the categorical imperative. And as stated before, that is and will continue to be a slow process because of logistical and financial issues as well as the time needed for attrition from an older generation of teachers who are not comfortable with technology to a younger generation that is. Also problematic with this change is the speed with which technology is changing. What works and can be implemented in the classroom today will be outdated in five years, thus perhaps requiring a different type of hardware, software, and the know-how to use them.

A second, and more heretical change involves the nature of curriculum itself. Most of the history of education in Western civilization has been backward focused -- a presentation of facts from the past. At the low end of the learning scale, facts are memorized and regurgitated. At the high end, they are analyzed and evaluated. Teaching historically happens in the "feeding a baby bird" style. Teachers select and chew up the material and then force-feed it into their students. But today's statistical and demographic evidence indicate that this method is having less and less effect on the Indigo mind. Students are simply not responding.

If, indeed, the Indigo structure is forward-focused, then the nature of curriculum needs to be redesigned to address that. And if Indigo children have the answers within themselves, then it follows that education needs to focus not on facts from the past, but on answers for the future. The way to access that is by asking questions, not giving answers. However, two great fears arise from this line of thought. The first is the fear of letting go of what has worked for two thousand years. Clearly it is impractical to "dump" what we have, and obviously, that is not the intent. But using the current political trend of recitation, application, and testing of facts is not working, and it is not enough. The downward spiral of education today needs a complete overhaul, not the continued refinement of assessment and an increasingly politicized national curriculum.

The second great fear is that Indigo answers might not match our facts. What could this look like? The fields of physics or astronomy are easy places to begin. New discoveries every day add to our knowledge base and often threaten pre-existing theories and philosophies. Catalyst and Conceptualist children today will be the future scientists who plumb the depths of these fields, and they will discard old theories without a second glance. It is possible that within themselves, even as children at some level, they realize that absorbing vast amounts of data today that will be useless tomorrow is a waste of their time. This attitude can happen in other areas as well. Art and literature of today are changing rapidly. Rap music alone is re-creating what poetry looks like and how it is used. Graphic novels have stormed the literary scene, combining text and images into storytelling. Certainly reading has become less focused on linear sequential absorption of information and moved to a self-selected system of movement through vast amounts of information chunked into visual appeal and occasional random connections. Tomorrow's children cannot tolerate the slowness or single focus of yesterday's presentation. New classics that the Artists will create may be delivered in new formats that do not even exist yet.

The best idea seems for today lies in an attempt to move education curriculum development to a middle ground, using fact for skill acquisition and practice, but allowing students ample opportunity *every single day* for questioning creatively, for synthesizing their own ideas into existing materials, and for hypothesizing possible alternatives to today's answers. These moments of the day give value to what is already in an Indigo child's mind as opposed to a current system that allows no space for this.

A third, and also heretical change also must happen to reengage the Indigo child in current education. That is to allow the student a vote in his own educational process, beginning at the elementary or primary level. Many Indigos are now like the child in the vignette at the beginning of this chapter who have an innate knowledge of what they can learn and when is the best time to learn it. Some day when Indigo young adults become teachers and administrators, the field of education will begin to allow even young children to pace themselves through their skill development via a choice of learning method and environment. This change will, unfortunately, take time and may develop at the expense of many of today's children.

Lack of a lock-step structure does not mean lack of learning, however. Indigos are willing to master material and go along willingly with a sensible plan. It would be a better format for Indigo learning if they had greater freedom, more choices, and more relaxed timing around their day. The concept of flex time has caught on in many workplaces, and adult Indigos function well in this environment. Children can thrive here too.

Like parents, teachers need to realize that communication is an all-important key with the Indigos. They must change the old paradigm that teachers talk and students listen. They also need to work with the fact that hyperactivity is neither abnormality nor misbehavior. The classroom of the future should be an active one in which students are encouraged to be outstanding and engaged at their own challenge level and pace, unlike classes today which homogenize students and learning. Classrooms should allow for movement and independence. Ideally, there should be a wide variety of independent projects, which allow student and teacher equal sharing of information and in which the learning process has variety and complexity. This can and should happen all the way through formal education, even in college and professional schools.

Prior to the advent of the Indigos, most students normally thought verbally or visually, not both. The Indigo Humanist and Artist work with both. When they listen to something, they are forming pictures and sentences conceptually and simultaneously. *Words plus images* equals reading for them. Anything else bores them and does not compute as well in their brain. Therefore, they require more time to process information than others. But once they have it, they never forget. Teachers must allow for this extra time in presenting new information and concepts. The Humanist and the Artist may seem slow while they are processing; they just need extra time to meld the words and pictures inside their minds. The Conceptualist and Catalyst do not have this dynamic.

Because the Indigo purpose is to advance civilization through technology, those students who come from backgrounds where technology is only marginally available in their home or early schooling, will suffer. Some futurists already call the poverty of the future that of technological deprivation. They speak of the gulf between those who know and use technology proficiently and creatively and those who have little access or savvy. Their only chance to do well for themselves is to break out of their environment.

Technology savvy applies to every kind of technology. Basics certainly include keyboard skills, presentation software, spreadsheets, word processing and publishing software, gaming, media literacy, and much experience with browsing and utilizing the Internet proficiently. Students need to practice and learn citing and giving credit to their sources early on. As students advance, they need to be exposed to safe practices of participatory sites where they can blog or post their thoughts and ideas and receive actual, real-world feedback.

And all that is just today! An almost immediate tomorrow calls for students to be able to read or watch quickly and absorb vast amounts of information from many types of media and to organize and use the information in their own creative ways. They will need to discern the agendas of information creators and be able to evaluate the credibility and reliability of that information. They will have to be proficient at knowing and understanding that information changes daily and to seek out the most valuable updates. They will then have to utilize their own natural creativity to read, write, and create new media products that they can post for others to see, respond to, and learn from. Critical thinking and problem solving need to occur *with technology*, not in isolation from it

As time goes by, proficient students will become involved with advanced gaming, virtual reality programs, and with creating and writing their own software and design systems. Indigos can and will learn from each other much faster than today's teachers are willing or able to teach computer savvy to them. Today's media children are tomorrow's problem solvers. Indigo Conceptualists and Catalysts will use virtual games and software systems to work out global problems of hunger, disease, poverty, and weather disasters. They will definitely pull solutions from underexplored areas in our oceans and space. These are not wishful hypotheses. Gamers have already discovered the structure of an AIDS-like virus that scientists were unable to decipher alone. Gaming allows for creating realities and practicing hypotheses in virtual realities, setting up scenarios for scientists to then transport into laboratories for actual testing. This is really just the beginning of utilizing games and gaming devices for problem solving in reality.

Certainly, there are inherent dangers in wide use for many types of technology because young people do not always make wise choices. Educators today tread a landscape dotted with landmines as they try to work out a safe technology environment for students yet still provide enough know-how for young Indigos to master evolving technology, thus remaining competitive at school and the workplace where knowing and using many forms of technology are a basic criteria for entrance and placement.

In addition to the shifting sands of Indigo masculine and feminine energies, and in addition to the speed at which the Indigo mind processes information, there are also a few other differences between Indigos and other life color behaviors in school.

As Indigo children get older, they love to participate in sports or drama, but they play for their own accomplishment, not for the team's. They will not sacrifice their body just to win. Their sense of accomplishment comes from their own personal performance. Occasionally the team can win, but the Indigo will still feel remiss because his individual performance did not match his expectations. Indigos will perform for the good of the group, but their personal performance is based on their personal best, not the defeat of someone else.

Within the four types of Indigos in a class, Humanists are the most grounded and adapt best in the typical classroom today because they look for more facts to ground and structure their dreams. They are more likely to stay in school. They prefer group work and chances to interact with their peers in the classroom and out of it. Humanists are the least theoretical and philosophical of the four Indigo types. They anchor their ideas and concepts in the reality of today.

Humanist students resonate most closely to curriculum that is about people. They understand approaching history, literature, and science as a study of people. These students easily relate to biography, psychology, language, and other subjects where teachers use the concept of people to open the door to that area of study. Humanists are the least likely to conceptualize studies that are not linked to people and how people work. A Humanist also works well with teachers who are friendly, kid-oriented, and casual in the classroom. They fail to appreciate the instructor who distances himself from his class, either through his personality or his teaching strategies.

In terms of day to day work, Humanists are the least likely to keep careful account of what, where, and when work is due. They are the least likely to keep their materials neat and their work organized. They need parents and teachers who repeatedly instruct and reinforce the value of good organizational skills and who provide motivation and reward for developing them.

Humanists also have a tendency to exert more time and effort trying to evade homework than it would actually take to *do* the homework. They love "cheats" in their games -- any device where they think they can outwit the system. They will do homework backwards if they can. For example, they will look at the questions at the back of a chapter and then hunt for the answers within the chapter as opposed to reading it in a linear, sequential manner. Part of this is due to their innate nature to read from media, where they are allowed to move from topic to topic by their own choice. Another place they sabotage their own learning efforts with traditional material is that, as readers, they have a tendency to ignore punctuation, racing ahead from word to word as fast as possible. This often affects their comprehension rate and ability. These factors are direct results of their need for speed -- hurrying and rushing to complete a task, even one of their games, in order to match the rate of their thinking and perceptions.

Unlike the Humanists, Artists in the classroom prefer projects where they can be creative and put themselves into their project. Even in math or science they like to put their own identity into the work. Computer programs and student-created media products easily allow this kind of adaptation. They can work alone or in groups as long as they get an equal chance to show their talent and individuality.

Artists do not like being called down by teachers and can be difficult in the classroom. They think they do everything perfectly. Although they like to get along with everyone, if they are under stress, they withdraw and become very quiet. If this happens in a group project, they will choose to do their work alone. They won't hesitate to tell a teacher or other student if something is done incorrectly. This isn't rudeness in their mind; it's correction for the aesthetic quality of the final product. They like a neat, organized classroom and are willing to help the teacher keep it that way. They are capable of tattling on others, especially if the quality of their own work is jeopardized. Their work and materials will be neatly and methodically organized in whatever kind of system has the greatest aesthetic appeal to them -- not necessarily for the teacher. Artist students are happy to point out when a textbook or answer key has errors -- or when the teacher is wrong.

Artists understand and appreciate subjects that are approached as drama or performance. They resonate to history as a human drama, to people like Cleopatra and Napoleon who knew how to "stage" their world. Artists love teachers who are dramatic performers in the classroom. Any teaching strategy involving costumes, make-up, and staging turn the Artist student on -- even if it involves technology. Literature and social science can well adapt to the Artist's learning preference. Other subjects can still work if Artists are allowed to design their homework artistically or technically rather than just answer questions objectively. Artists will perform well on tests if they approach the testing concept as an opportunity to perform or if a reward is attached. They prefer tests that have an element of design involved.

Conceptualists in the classroom demand a completely different approach. They are much less personal and much less personable. Sometimes they can be difficult. They will not care anything for the dramatic approach of the Artist; in fact, that style will seem silly or uncomfortable to the Conceptualist. Nor will they resonate to the touchy-feely preferences of the Humanist. Conceptualists do not work as well with others. They are excellent at systems, conceptualizing the project as a whole, time management, and controlling the flow of a project. They prefer to be in charge. They will not tattle on others. However, they will sabotage those in the group who do not do their share of the work or who do not complete their project on time, cutting them out of the project entirely or asking the teacher to remove them from the project if they feel they cannot control the timing or over-all group effort. Conceptualists want control. They are the best at working with patterns and structure. They don't tattle; they just get rid of the problem at any cost.

Conceptualists can learn successfully from home schooling or from online classes as well. They like the consistency of computers and the opportunity to engage with technology, their genius factor. They also resonate to the fact that, at home, there is not as much time in the classroom spent on crowd control, social factors, or dysfunctional group work. Depending on their relationship with their parents, home schooling can work well for the Conceptualist student. This student can use extra time at home for deeper study of systems, structures, and topics of independent interest.

Catalysts in the classroom are often disruptive. Social graces and rules of group behavior do not always compute to them. If they have a question, they will just blurt it out or demand attention until their need is met. They just do not get group dynamics. Brilliant children, they are the most likely to be autistic. Some actually are, and some buy into the hype of autism in order to be left alone. For the last several years, Nancy has observed that about fifty percent of children labeled autistic actually *are* autistic. The other fifty percent pick up clues from their home, family, and school environments and use the label to their advantage. Being labeled autistic serves them well because people leave them alone or acquiesce to their strange behavior.

A solution for this seems to be for psychology and the behavioral sciences to continue refining and defining characteristics of true autism, treatments for it, and behavior modifications. Some school districts are now hiring Autism Coordinators to assist both students and teachers with their behavior and needs. In the last ten years, much progress has been made in this area. But there is no one simple answer. With some children diet modification is very effective; with others it does little good. Some autistic children (usually Humanists and Artists) respond well to systematic, structured behavior modifications seen today. The Catalysts just want to be left alone, and they adapt to behavior modification the least successfully.

In the classroom, Catalysts are the best at seeing the big picture, the global effects of a cause, or the development of something over a long period of time. They are capable of much greater abstract thought than the other students. Learning the fine details of a topic may have little or no appeal to them unless it is a subject that really ignites their particular interest. The Catalyst will physically be the largest child in class and often a loner. Attempts to integrate them into a group or the class as a whole are often in vain. They may be able to learn from a lecture hall type of presentation, a place where they can attend impersonally, absorb the information they want, and then leave, all without having to interact with anyone. Catalysts will also benefit from home schooling where their anti-social needs can be best addressed.

Indigos with a dual combination of Indigo types are luckier than others because they have twice the flexibility in their learning preferences and can appreciate and thrive with two types of classroom teacher styles instead of just one.

How will necessary changes happen in the education field? From young adult Indigos who become teachers. They themselves will understand and be able to create the education of the future. Certainly they already have a good start with technology because they are young enough to be in on the ground floor of the rapid growth in this area. Much more important, however, is that they intuit and understand Indigo learning needs: to be guided rather than instructed and to be encouraged to expand their natural curiosity and creativity rather than repress it.

What are Indigo teachers like in the classroom? The patterns are predictable. Humanists are the most casual, both liking their students and relating to them. Humanists in the classroom like to talk! They are the ideal lecturers, and class discussion is comfortable for them. They will easily understand the need to ask thoughtful questions and encourage their students to do likewise. They will use group activities and will be among the first to appreciate using social media and people-oriented, educational software programs. Shy students may easily benefit from a Humanist teacher who can draw them out and enfold them into classroom activities. This Indigo teacher will put a high value on classroom participation, give extra credit, and be available before and after school to talk to students and assist them as needed.

If students are looking for a dramatic presentation style, however, like the "sage on the stage," then they need to find an Artist for their instructor. The Artist teacher will bring drama, creativity, and an artistic approach to his classroom. This teacher will often be voted the best teacher on campus or the most popular teacher because of their presentation style. The classroom will be neat and attractive with the aesthetic appeal changed frequently to meet the Artist's every changing mood and unit material. An Artist teacher will like student assignments or tests featuring an oral presentation, group presentation, artistic project, or students who present plays, etc. They also may ask students to incorporate artistic elements into their media presentations, posters, or written work. Even spreadsheets can have artistic appeal and elements.

The Conceptualist Indigo as the classroom teacher is, once again, definitely different. This teacher is the *expert,* detached, fully in control of his subject, and often unconcerned with how students are faring in his subject. He or she is liable to have occasional difficulties with students who challenge classroom control or the teacher's air of superiority, something teenagers love to do. However, this teacher really is an authority. He will be the one on campus to understand and use technology the most and will be eager to impart that knowledge to students. The Conceptualist is the best at assessment, loving to create and interpret assessment data, the best systems of assessment for student progress, and the best use of technology to evaluate student work objectively. Conceptualists are also the best asset to have on campus to know what new technology is just around the corner to help students take the next step into the future.

Catalysts are unlikely to be in the classroom unless they are guest lecturers, research professors, or instructors who have little or no contact with their actual students. A Catalyst might work successfully with podcasts or remote teaching where they do not have to put in a public appearance at all. They could also become "virtual teachers," designing and developing formats that deliver material without human contact. With the kinds of virtual reality programs that already exist, students simulate possible solutions to problems, challenge their conceptual understandings of classroom material, and create new solutions to existing problems.

Teachers who are dual Indigo types have twice the likelihood of relating to a wider variety of Indigo students. Indigo teachers do not merge their types nor dilute their ability to use either type as a teaching tool. They are just twice as talented.

What is the likelihood of an ideal world where Humanist children will always draw Humanist teachers to learn from? None. Over the course of an education, children and teachers of every Indigo type will interact with each other time and time again. But even a relatively basic system of identification such as Nancy provides can help each of them identify each other. A Humanist student can say, "Uh, oh, I've got a Conceptualist teacher for math," and then plot a compensating strategy for that semester. In an ideal world some day, Conceptualist teachers will know that many of their students will be Humanists and will need more personal contact and support than they (teachers) are always comfortable with. Knowledge is power. Even simple strategies and awareness of the four types and their styles can go a long way with Indigo learners and teachers.

For school administrators of the future, it is important to realize that Indigos work best in a system of rules that are not absolute and non-negotiable. The Indigo instinctive nature under that kind of system is to react negatively and to rebel. Education of the future will look like a fluid system of individualized choice and progression. Teachers will also need much greater freedom to assist students with their own natural expertise instead of having to put so much time and effort into presentation and grading. As one administrator put it, "For the last two years, I prefer to replace retiring teachers with young adults whose tech skills outweigh their academic criteria. Teachers sort out their expertise and interest among themselves. Everything gets covered, but in a different way."

Students will approach skill acquisition and study of "chunks" of curricular material through their choice of media approach or learning strategy, depending on how they learn best or their state of readiness at the time. All curricular material will be a combination of words and images. Students will be trained in asking questions, not just supplying answers learned in a system of rote memorization. Virtual teachers and virtual classrooms are already possible and available through a variety of websites. Colleges, businesses, and individuals utilize the learning potential and creativity offered in these sites. There needs to be a "filter down" process with teachers and curriculum developers willing to adapt these to middle and high school use today, and eventual elementary or primary use tomorrow.

Schools themselves will change. Today the education field is still locked into the mindset of schools and school districts as distinct entities, each from the other. A small town in Kansas has a complete school district with separate buildings for each age grouping of students. In the next small town in Kansas there is another district with distinct and separate buildings for each age grouping of students -- and so on around the world. Schools have been created and run in the same assembly line process that students have been. There is no sharing of resources, talent, equipment, or solutions from one small town to another. The curriculum that is taught in one school is exactly replicated in the next one just a few miles down the road. Indigos will change this. They will bring about a globalized education process where, even in rural areas, small towns will share resources with their neighbors, thus being able to use teacher resources more effectively and to offer more diverse opportunities for student learning. In urban areas the ability to spread and multiply resources is far greater using interlinked media and technology.

Today we are still in the middle of the storm that Indigos have brought about to tear down the centuries-old education system. Too many students have been caught up in the debris of escalating drop-out rates and disengagement in the current classroom. However, it is also the Indigos themselves that are the rainbow behind the clouds, showing us how the rebirth and renewal of education will happen when didactic is combined with media and technology, when student curiosity and creativity drive curriculum, and when students have an active voice in their own learning process.

In the best of all possible worlds today, how then is it then possible to teach students in a classroom containing all four types of Indigo? Get rid of the textbook or use it as a supplement. Move faster. Put students on computers, tablets, and phones for both knowledge acquisition and testing. In developing countries some of this may happen directly from cell phones -- any form of technology that is visual, graphic, and fast. Let students work alone or with a partner or small group. Open the door to an idea or concept to explore and establish some learning goals. Provide initial sources of information and then encourage them to investigate further, using specifically identified criteria for what types of information are useful and acceptable. Let them have a voice in what kind of media presentations or formats to create for their products.

Test them as often as necessary for comprehension, making sure that the students have access to and understand the testing feedback results. Be available as a resource, both academically and technically for student questions and problems. Allow students to help and advance each other. Keep their focus on questions and investigations, not "right" answers. Allow and encourage them to bring their own creativity and talent to the learning endeavor. Watch them soar!

10

Indigos at Work

*C*huck *is in charge of creative development projects at a software design firm. He oversees several projects at once. A new endeavor has been approved for the first stage of development, and Chuck will now assemble the team to get things rolling. He is sure he wants Robb, whose technical skill is legendary in the field and whose leadership as a taskmaster is a valuable asset. Chuck is torn between Syndi, talented but occasionally hard to work with, and Louann, a good artist but lacking in pure creativity. He chooses Syndi, thinking that he can watch her carefully and dodge the minefield of her moods. Finally, he adds Paul to the mix, counting on Paul's writing skills and easy-going nature. Chuck does not know it, but he has assembled an Indigo dream team. Brilliant, creative, and talented, they will work together to give Chuck the kind of product he envisions.*

Throughout most of mankind's history, a young boy never wondered what he would become as he grew up. No one ever asked him, "what do you want to be when you grow up?" He already knew. He would be what his dad was. If Dad farmed, he farmed. After the Industrial Revolution, if Dad worked in a factory, he worked in a factory. Sometimes a second or third son had the freedom to look elsewhere, perhaps the church or military, but first and second sons were essential to perpetuate the present and take it into the future. Girls were necessary for cooking, housework, and child raising. They began their own monotonous sequence when they were in their teens. Life for most people on earth was one of survival and replication. The education necessary for life began in childhood and on site. Boys helped Dad, and girls helped Mom. All too often, Mom died young, and the oldest girls were suddenly drafted into immediate service themselves. This life still exists in developing countries.

But another kind of life is supplanting it in industrial nations. When Indigo children began appearing in the 1960's and 1970's, computers were in their infancy and only belonged to very large businesses or universities. The personal computer did not exist. The Internet had not been created per se. In fact, in 1993, less than two percent of existing information on earth was telecommunicated. Today that number is more than 97%. When the first Indigos appeared, social media and virtual realities did not exist, nor had anyone even dreamed of them. There were no mobile devices. If one wanted to use the phone, he had to go to a place where a phone was located. There were few computer programmers in existence, no video game developers, no social media managers, no IT managers, and no virtual personal assistants located in Bangalore. In other words, the first Indigos came into a world where the jobs they would have in their adult lives did not even exist. That is the new pattern for Indigo children born today. They will grow up, pursue an education and training for, and work in jobs which may not exist today, and if they do, which will look vastly different than they do now.

Before the Indigos, children in industrialized nations were born, studied, and then spent their life working. Those who were lucky or healthy or both, then retired and lived out their lifespan. Today's children will be born, study, and then work some, study some, work some more, play some, study some, work some more, and play some more. Their life cycle of productivity may not occur on a Bell Curve at all; instead, it may evolve in irregular cycles, continuing long past today's retirement age. Marriages and relationships may look similar, but that is the subject matter for the next chapter.

As a culture we have not had very long to adjust to new ways of doing things. The Indigos themselves have had almost no time. The work world they found on entry looked hostile: formal, top-down management in old, established bureaucratic systems, fixed and rigid work times and environments, and little time during the day for socializing. Gender roles were clearly defined and seldom discussed. Men made decisions.

Men and women implemented them. Men ran the corporate world; men ruled the non-profit world and women implemented their suggestions. Hierarchical structures were seldom challenged, and there were few formal processes for workplace iniquities.

Clearly this was not a working world where Indigos would be comfortable based on what Nancy has perceived of their personality patterns. And while Indigos are not responsible for initiating the social changes that have relaxed work environments and provided more equitable work conditions for males and females, nevertheless, they (Indigos) are making their mark and changing how work happens and how we feel about how work should happen.

It is essential to remember that since Indigos became teenagers, every social choice they make involves the risk of death. Drinking and drugs, unchecked, can lead to overdose and death. Pregnancy and abortion can run amok. The dangers of early and unchecked sex can lead to AIDS, STDs, and other diseases. Any combination of the above only exacerbates the chances of negative consequences. Their video games are filled with violence, as are the movies and television shows they have watched since they were small children. They have a clear certainty that their families, churches, schools, and governments cannot guarantee their safety through life. Consequently, they live for today, and they work for themselves.

What then do they bring to the workplace in terms of attitude? The obvious answer is change. Let's start with their natural talent: technology. The Indigos themselves will evolve naturally and simultaneously with technology. As they invent new technologies, they will create new jobs for themselves, releasing old structures for yet newer forms. Their intuitive interest in and talent for new applications of what technology can do will drive business of the future. The Indigos have already begun to and will continue to globalize the world -- in business, medicine, banking and economy, education, travel, communication, and even in how we deliver our goods and services on a local level. They will use virtual realities to create actual realities. They will protect and defend with more and more sophisticated tools and weaponry. They will explore with increasingly complex machinery, both in space and under the seas.

They will simulate their trial and error refinements, reducing time and minimizing costs. More and more tasks will be automated. But none of this is new news. We can easily see the beginnings of these technology implications in the lives of Indigos today.

The Indigos are just getting started making changes. The demographics of the workplace are changing enormously. Today Caucasians are rapidly losing their majority. Figures change too rapidly to insert percentages, but know that by 2025, most decision makers around the world will be young, female, and brown. Due to the androgynous energy of the Indigo, women will outnumber men in some of the less creative fields. Many Indigos will be single parents, and as a consequence, work decisions they make will, by necessity, often be related to the health and welfare of their children. Many will live on one continent and work on another one. Some will not have a work place at all; their productivity will happen in a variety of locations and will be interlinked to people they know personally or those in faraway places that they will never meet.

Indigos will not think in terms of their career as a singular entity; they think of themselves as *resume builders*. They take and give up jobs easily, preferring to add or subtract positions that enhance themselves as individuals and that enable them to add new skills or interests. They may choose to float from the for-profit sector to the non-profit sector, depending again on their global interests and the creativity they can bring to a project. They look for each job to give them the opportunity to expand their skill base, to provide them an opportunity to be creative, and to give them the means to live the lifestyle they like. They do not think their work is their life, nor do they identify themselves by their job. They are individuals. Work is one of the things that they do.

Nor will they believe in corporate loyalty. Today's Indigos do not believe that they will be taken care of in their old age by a company or government system or that they must sacrifice their values or lives for that company or system. Again, they live for today. Consequently, they demonstrate these values in the attitude they bring to work as employees. They consider a work day what their contract says. When the contract says their day is over, they leave, whether the task is done or not. This is especially true for the Humanists. When their three month or six month evaluation is due, they expect a raise and a promotion, whether the quality of their work warrants it or not. They are not shy about asking for the same rate of escalation as their peers, again whether the quality of their work measures up or not. If, and this is remarkable, they actually do as much or more work as their boss, and the boss takes credit for it (something that has always happened,) the Indigo will make that known and expect reward for it. All these behaviors are clear examples of their sense of entitlement. The Indigo concept of "right to work" means "right to work my way." They expect acknowledgement and reward through their presence, not through their achievement.

To those of us who are older or not Indigo, these expectations are remarkable, and sometimes appalling. We had to earn our way. They just expect theirs to happen. We judge them as not having a work ethic. Nancy sees it differently. To her, it is a matter of focus and perspective.

Let's look at each type of Indigo. Humanists are social. Work provides an opportunity for them to globalize the world and to connect humans everywhere. When they are in a position that they can utilize their social media devices, work in groups, communicate freely with others, and contribute to the good of the whole, they are happy. The culture of a working environment is critically important to them. If they need to work overtime on a project, it is best then for the manager to make the event look as social as possible. Humanists who are unhappy at work or not particularly successful in their jobs are those who are restricted from communicating freely with others, who do not have enough time to socialize with their peers, or those whose social life outside of work is so valuable to them that they will risk work time to maintain and nurture it. They can be whistle-blowers if their social process is jeopardized or if their self-esteem is threatened by their peers. A wise manager will do whatever is necessary to restore the Humanist's equilibrium by encouraging him or her to take a break, take some time by himself, and then to come and talk things over. Talking is the Humanist's therapy. Even if an ultimate decision goes against the Humanist, the fact that he or she got to present his point of view and was listened to is what counts.

On the other hand, Artists will work tirelessly and long, long hours to perfect their art. They will endanger their health if necessary. But the task has to be about *them -- their art, their design, their creation.* They will strive to get along with the group until the aesthetic value of the project is compromised. They do not mind being whistle-blowers or running to a supervisor about the productivity of a co-worker, especially if the action makes the Artist look more special or if product integrity is compromised. If there is a dramatic incident going on in the workplace, look for the Artist to be the creative force behind it. They bring their daily drama to work with them each and every day.

Artists are fastidious with their work as well as their work space. In retail work or in a work environment where presentation is important, the wise manager will put an Artist in charge. He will also realize that criticism does not work well at all. The Artist believes he or she has done the work perfectly because *in their artistic vision,* it was perfect. Artists worry about their social standing. It is important that their job title be perceived as important.

Reprimanding them or criticizing them is tricky. If they feel the criticism is unwarranted, they will just zone out; in their minds they will justify their actions to themselves and see the manager as wrong. Being super-sensitive, they can cry easily and often. In a negative mood, they will play victim. They will also turn the reprimand into a *big drama.* The manager needs to realize that everything with the Artist is a *big drama.* The best way for a manager of an Indigo Artist to turn his or her emotions around is to get back to their design and creative process.

The Indigo Conceptualist is a different matter altogether. They are the *geeks* and *nerds* (of either gender) who work tirelessly on their project. They are designers, engineers, and builders who find answers. They are project-driven at all times. Technical geniuses, they take things apart, both physically and metaphorically, often putting them back together differently but better. The most methodical of all the four types of Indigo, the Conceptualist is just that -- the idea person. Other than the Catalyst, they are the least social, preferring to work alone. They will often think the social aspects of work are unimportant and can resent the time taken away from their project. They do not necessarily understand tact or the necessity for either finessing a social situation or the nuances of human behavior. This is fine when they work alone in a cubicle. But once they advance to a team scenario or management position, the task of managing people can often lead a Conceptualist completely out of his comfort zone until he or she can analyze the situation and see people management as just another system to master. They work behind the scenes better than their fellow Humanists or Artists.

Conceptualists can work tirelessly as long as they are working on their project. They are the ones who work well from home, something the Humanists do not find social enough. Conceptualists also work well from an airplane, airport lounge, their car, or Starbucks. In truth, their computer is their workplace. It does not matter where the computer is situated physically.

When Conceptualists determine whether or not to take a new job, they should ask about existing technology and budgets for whatever type of technology they might need for their work. While Artists care about the social status of their position or the aesthetics of their performance venue, Conceptualists focus on being able to be in control of their project or on being superior to those they work with. They care about the hardware and software they want, need, and use. They care about their timeline and project control. Most of all, they care about being in a position where they are in control and can maintain superiority over their own domain, however it is defined.

Conceptualists who feel stress from work are those who are asked to perform socially, who are not given enough time to analyze a situation thoroughly, or who feel they have lost control. A wise manager will get them back to their project and work to assure them that they are still in control.

Today, the Indigo Catalyst is still so rare and socially dysfunctional that he is really not a workplace factor. This Indigo type can look like the autistic savant who must be managed in almost a one-on-one situation, where his knowledge and expertise are extracted and used by others. The Catalyst will project an air of complete superiority and abstraction. However, as time evolves, they will be the ones who bring great solutions, great philosophies, and answers for mankind's biggest problems. They will be the ones who see a need for universal change; they will have the vision necessary to bring it about.

Some young Indigo adults have not been able to find their way in the work world at all. A variety of factors have created this. For some, they graduated with a degree or certificate for which there was no job market when they finished. Others never found a field that "felt right." Still others just cannot seem to find the internal motivation to progress beyond their parents' couch at home. Some are addicted to their video games and unwilling to face an actual work day away from them. Many Indigos cannot envision work the way their father did, endless years of hard labor with little reward after the gold watch. Stuck in neutral, many have tuned out for so long during their education that they are now unable to move into the job market because they lack basic skills. These young Indigos have been caught up in the storm of change in our culture today and have been unable to find the resources to adapt to new circumstances. They have chosen to become hapless victims of changing times rather than rebirthing themselves for the future. In their way they are also making the Indigo statement: old ways no longer work. The individual of the future will not work in the way of the past.

As young Indigos today continue to make their surge into the workplace, it is important to remember their overriding values: globalized interconnectedness, technology, and working together for the good of all. Wise supervisors, like Chuck, will be those who talk to them, who take an interest in an Indigo's life, world, and values, and who coach and mentor them rather than directing them authoritatively. Indigos like to be acknowledged for their contributions, and they like being respected for their values. It is not necessary for everyone else to have the same values -- just acknowledge their point of view. The wise manager also has to know that the Indigo will confront his hypocrisy, challenge inequity in the workplace, and demand a raise all on the same day.

11

Love, Indigo Style

*P*icture this. *A pretty high school senior is sharing her scrapbook with the class. As she turns from one creatively crafted page to another, she narrates, "This was my boyfriend when I was in 9th grade. He dumped me." She turns the page and continues, "This was my boyfriend in 10th grade. Here are our pictures of the dance in the fall and when we went to Disneyland. Then he dumped me." She moves on to the 11th grade saying, "This was my boyfriend. You really can't see him because I cut him out of the picture. He dumped me too. I liked the picture of myself though so I left my half in." Once again she turns the page, "This was my boyfriend last fall but we are going to different colleges and won't see each other so I dumped him." The class breaks into spontaneous applause, and a scattering of female hands pump the air.*

Clearly romance is not what it used to be. The young woman in this vignette has swiftly and efficiently recounted her high school love life with detachment and clarity. She is ready to move on. The reader can imagine from all the previous chapters that if Indigos do things differently in every other area of life, they will most certainly demonstrate their independence and free thinking in their relationships. Indigos today use social media to announce to the world that they are "in a relationship" or "no longer in a relationship." Cultural anthropologists might view that as a status indicator for those in the hunt, but it is most likely that the Humanists are just keeping their peers up to date, and the Artists want someone to feel their pain. Conceptualists might not have been aware that they were in a relationship until they were notified via their own social media site. All kidding aside, this is the material of today's sitcoms on television and in movies. Watch them to view how Indigos value each other as dating potential, mating potential, or most important, just friends. Young Indigo females propose to their guy friends or just bypass the entire process if they are ready to have a child; they visit a sperm bank and move forward. Recent newspaper accounts are peppered with articles about "donor parents" and "donor siblings" having reunions. Destination weddings are really about the party, not about the "joining together of this man and this woman." They already did that, a long time ago. Today's Indigo has an increasing resistance to sacrifice who they are for environmental training.

But believe it or not, the married Indigo today also has a greater capacity for true and real love than those in previous generations. Indigos prefer being friends first, and often best friends. For them true love is a combination of companionship plus passion. The real concerns in an Indigo marriage are trust, honesty, and friendship. They are willing to work through their issues and try to solve them. If that does not work, however, they will abandon their partner and move on to a better one. Indigos do not tolerate repression in their relationships, nor will they stay in one for the sake of children, religious values, or money.

First and foremost, they believe in clear communication. Negotiation and bribery are absolutely successful, especially if those techniques keep the marriage dynamic balanced and fair. Indigos share the work load as a family, dividing up the daily task of living equally, with each partner taking those tasks he or she prefers or is best at. They can always swap later. In a successful Indigo marriage, both partners will often work efficiently through tasks so the maximum amount of free time can be spent in "hanging out." That can look like an evening out with friends, climbing a mountain, studying together, or cooking at home. In western cultures, theirs will never be the "big man" and "little woman" type of relationship that has prevailed in previous generations, nor will Indigos allow one partner to have a bigger vote than the other. They live and work side by side as partners, and each is capable of having good friends among both genders. Many young married adults today look forward to their "guys" weekend or a "girls" weekend, with each of them going their separate ways for a couple of days to be with friends. Neither partner is threatened by this time spent apart. Both know they will each have the same opportunity later.

Because Indigos are open and honest in their communication, they have a much better chance for a successful and happy marriage. However, this does not automatically infer that it will be one which lasts for fifty years. Because of the rapid pace of today's world and the speed with which Indigos process their lives, they can and do experience more in five years of a relationship than our great grandparents did in fifty years. It will become more and more common for a happy Indigo couple to decide to re-commit or not re-commit to another span of time together. Some may just decide they need to move on, perhaps choosing a job in another city or deciding to go back to school somewhere else. They can and often do remain close friends for the rest of their lives. Paperwork can always be changed. The magic, however, is that the love remains -- in an Indigo way. Their love is already forever.

Indigos do not enjoy dating per se. They prefer meeting and sorting through the first stages of a relationship by "hanging out" with friends, both male and female. They much prefer that to the formal, and occasionally strained, conventions of dating. Often they utilize their natural resource (technology) to optimize the hunt, seeking, sorting through, and finding potential kindred spirits as efficiently as possibly via a dating website. They can get text, visual input, and an initial interaction immediately and in a much less threatening scenario than the tension of a "blind date" or bar scene.

Indigos do not get married to have sex. They view sex as a fun, biological function, separate from morals or ethics. For them the body is a play toy. Their heart is not connected to a body part. They will not marry just for the sake of a conceived child, nor will they stay together for one either. This is in no way to infer that Indigos do not have moral or ethical values. They absolutely do, and they believe their values to be clearer and more honest than all previous generations. They strongly believe in love. They do not link it to sex though, nor do they believe in using sex to justify partnering.

Indigos have managed to integrate technology into their sex lives, and conversely, sex into technology, with creativity and humor. Phone sex is common and useful when couples work in different locations. "Sexting" (sending text messages with sexual content) is also common, as is posting one's sexual profile online. As mentioned in Chapter 2, pornography abounds. In some countries it is the number one use of Internet search engines. Indigos are open and honest about these practices; they assume everyone knows about them and does the same.

How do the different types of Indigo approach their relationships? Indigo Humanists will be monogamous and loyal in a relationship as long as it is positive and healthy. They are real with those they love. Humanists couples can talk about everything. Friends first, last, and always, they each value the opinions of their mate and know that feelings are reciprocated. They keep in constant touch, utilizing every form of technology to register their actions and progress through the day, and to manage their daily life efficiently. Depending on their environmental training, two Humanists together may place a low value on housekeeping, preferring time spent together on more social activities.

Humanists are sensitive in their relationships. They fear rejection and betrayal, so any action on the partner's behalf that looks like these negative behaviors is a definite threat to the Humanist's well-being and the health of the relationship. A Negative Humanist will cheat, seeking out someone else to socialize with or someone else who shows potential for another relationship. Or they spend more time with their "buddies" or peer group than with their partner. Open, honest communication is the key for Humanists to resolve potential conflicts or to reach a mutual decision to move on and go their separate ways.

Indigo Artists perform their emotions in their relationship. An Artist's partner must be prepared for the drama and the continual "maintenance" needed to keep the Artist in equilibrium such as sacrificing closet space for the shoes. Artists are expensive to live with because of their need for "the best." They also are capable of putting their relationship on hold, leaving the partner at home and alone, while the Artist puts in long hours perfecting his or her craft. Artists need to be reassured by their partner that they are loved and needed. The Indigo Artist has the greatest capability of bringing joy and laughter to any partnership because of his or her own exuberance and lightness of being.

The flaw an Artist brings to a relationship is his or her ego. Artists believe they are right, so seeing the other person's point of view is nearly impossible for them without work and communication. Artists need a partner who appreciates and shares their need to keep a neat, clean environment at all times. An Artist who brings negative energy to a relationship will cause drama! Artists are the most likely Indigo type to do something sneaky or hidden behind the partner's back, even if they do not consider it serious. They will also be the most earnest in their denial of this action. Parting will always be tearful and dramatic.

Conceptualists in a relationship will work to bring positive energy, trying to control and "manage" their relationship. They will be positive as long as their work or hobby projects are progressing well. In other words, work can often come first. If relationship problems do come up, the Conceptualist will attempt to analyze and examine them from every angle. But the Conceptualist's drawbacks in a relationship can be serious. Their very asset can also be their undoing. They devote tireless time and energy to their current project, often sacrificing equal time and effort for devotion to their partner. A Conceptualist's partner can often feel like wallpaper in the relationship, unnoticed and unappreciated. Conceptualists themselves can also be completely unaware of the feelings of their partner.

Conceptualists working from home are no more attached to their relationship than if they went to a job in a cubicle every day. They require a separate work space in the house. Once they are there, their mind is completely removed from the thought of home, family, and personal life. Even aside from their work life, Conceptualists can often become involved in their games or media which can cause them to disconnect from family life as well.

In theory, a Conceptualist makes the ideal home repair partner because of his or her ability to take apart a system needing maintenance, correct the situation, and then put it back together. Conceptualists can figure out anything; however, this is not always the case. Some Conceptualists are so devoted to their technology or project that anything related to daily life, like making coffee or repairing a broken hinge, is completely baffling.

A Negative Conceptualist or one who is ready to leave a relationship will sabotage the relationship, dump his or her partner without explanation, or just move out. Conceptualists can also bury themselves in their project or gaming device and tune their former partner out. When it is time to go, the Conceptualist will break something, figuratively or literally. This should be a sign to the partner that this relationship is done.

Indigo Catalysts can also have positive relationships if they are built around the Catalyst's cause or vision. Catalysts are loyal to their cause, not necessarily to a person. Any relationship that fits within that cause can be successful. Joint research partners or a couple devoted to a philanthropic service can make a successful partnership for Catalysts as long as both people are focused on their vision. Their conversation, free time, and efforts must remain about their work together or their view of the future. If a relationship falters, the Catalyst cannot repair it because he or she does not know how it started to begin with. They do not have the mechanism to understand or analyze an emotional process.

It is essential to understand about Indigo energy and the young people who bring Indigo energy to life today, that love is a qualitative value, not a quantitative one. Love does not equal time. Indigos do not gain or lose love. They share love, treasuring it while it is actively expressed and then retaining the qualities of it when time moves them to another experience. This is a difficult concept to grasp for those of us who do not have an Indigo life color. When it comes to love, it seems that Indigos have broken every cultural and religious value that generations before them have taken as moral imperatives. Indigos have stormed the bastion of our beliefs, unwilling to take on our hypocrisy or our decision to endure a dysfunctional relationship for the sake of social or family pressures.

The Indigo ability to love is genuine, whole, and integral to their very being. It is not performance according to cultural values or tradition. Love is not behavior, nor is it a timeline. Instead Indigos today show us the love of tomorrow and the joy it holds for everyone. We can all gain from what they have to teach us in this area if we maintain a constant and intense curiosity about and acceptance for love, Indigo style.

12

To Indigos Today
and Tomorrow

To my dear Indigo friends around the globe, welcome. It has been a privilege and a pleasure to share space with you, to get to know you, and to watch and feel your energy and enthusiasm. Many of you have come to me in the last few years asking for advice about getting through these changing times successfully. I will tell you what I can.

First, try to stay centered. Even with the winds of chaos and revolution swirling around you, be at peace within yourself. You are neither warrior, nor peacemaker. You are social creatures who show your gifts and talents early and proudly. You are bright, and you feel you have the right to put your thoughts, ideas, talents, indeed, your very self out into the world. You produce through action. Consequently, when you feel stymied and unable to move, then that is your internal monitor requesting that you replenish and refresh before you begin again. Be at peace with yourself and who you are.

What should you do to stay centered? Take one day at a time. When you feel most uncertain about yourself and your desires, use your greatest tool: the media. Tune into the media you love. Look for a new game, a new form of social media, or a new software program that intrigues and delights you. Watch television, play your games with friends, use your social media venues, listen to your music. Text, blog, and post your thoughts. But even more important, learn to be a voyeur, an observer of the trends in your own personal pop culture. See what your brother and sister Indigos are doing.

Watch people your age when you go out. Whether you go to the zoo, the airport, or a music venue, watch the people. Listen to them talk. What trends do you see and hear? How do you fit in to those trends? Are your tastes changing or growing more solid? Do fewer people like your music or your games? If so, what changes are they making?

Watch young people in the media and then ask yourself some questions. What are they doing that is new? Does that resonate to you? Is change happening around you, and is it leaving you behind, or is it time for you to move on and leave it behind? Do not be afraid to do either. As you watch or participate in the media you love most, ask yourself how you can apply what you are seeing and experiencing to your own life. Are you learning or just biding your time? Are you acquiring talents or just zoning out? What in your life creates a need for you to zone out? Are you running away? What do you need to run away from? Are you happy? Is your world functioning?

What do you need to do within yourself to create happiness? What do you want most in your life right now? Or what would you like your life to look like in five years that you could begin right now?

Look within yourself for the answers to these questions because that is where you will find them. Then notice the difference between the answer you find within yourself and where you see your life right now. What needs to happen to bring the two things closer together? Who in your world are you listening to and agreeing or disagreeing with? Take the necessary action you feel is right for you. If necessary, distance yourself from your environment or from your peer group. It might not need to be permanent. You might just need a break.

Be ready to change at any moment because you are going to. How do you view yourself when you are alone? How do you see yourself amidst a crowd? Are you comfortable with yourself? Are you comfortable with others? If not, what do you want to do about that?

Many Indigos have asked me about love. I tell them that Indigos see a wholeness that the rest of us do not see. Love is the art of living. Your idea of love has no beginning and no end. Your physical relationships may come and go, but the love stays. Indigos are like a chain adding new loops with each relationship. They are the chain, never broken, always adding more people to love and more memories to share.

Enjoy love. You can't plan it. You can't hang onto it. You can build on it. And at the end, it will slip away. It is more important to enjoy love than to try to hold on forever without enjoyment. For you, love is friendship plus passion. Neither can exist without the other.

You have asked me about God and how to find God. I say, look within yourselves. Find your own definition of God. You may wish to share that definition within a church or religious organization, or you may not. Don't be afraid to be yourself. Morality is perspective.

In the worst of times, breathe. It keeps you alive. As long as you are alive, you can work something out. Breathing is the first step to everything.

And finally, don't take it too serious.

Nancy

These words directly from Nancy Tappe are to those Indigos everywhere who have pioneered new ideas, new ways of doing things, and new behavior patterns. There is no doubt about it. The Indigo storm of energy and influence has swept the globe, bringing change at every level and in every area of man's existence. The center of the storm is globalization, a social change born on the winds of technology. It is creating the *one world, one people* that Indigos came to bring about. Within the next forty years as Indigos begin to come into their power as adults, the emphasis will be even stronger in favor of one world, not one country or one political power. Countries will each retain their individual character, philosophical nature, and regional interests. They will focus more on improving social problems at home than has happened previously. Indigos are keenly aware of social inequalities within their own countries and are eager to tackle these problems in ways that are less politicized.

We see early harbingers of this one world already. It is easy today to envision the advent of one humanitarian force coming together for peace keeping missions or crisis management and control after a tsunami, hurricane, or monsoon. We already live in one world in medicine where an x-ray can be taken in America or Europe, interpreted in India, a collaborative diagnosis and treatment decided on via web conferencing with doctors in several countries, and then discussed with the patient over a cell phone. Businessmen and politicians in the United States or Europe today use personal assistants in India to manage their social agendas, to take care of routine business, and to prepare speeches and media presentations. The corporate world already embraces the efficiency and cost effectiveness of manufacturing in a developing country, shipping its products via container ships that move from continent to continent, and then using automated systems to load, move, deliver, and unload goods and materials to its retail outlets or vendors for local delivery.

The worlds of science, media, and technology are daily explosions of development with each new update or development fueling the one that comes immediately after. Experts in those areas interface and work together with colleagues around the globe, many of whom they have never met. Scientists will soon share honors and awards for scientific breakthroughs, having worked collegially yet never even been in the same country at the same time.

Males and females are beginning to re-evaluate their life goals, their priorities, and their interests. Men are beginning to feel the need to be more creative, more focused on home, family, and creative ventures. Women are becoming more energized by the business world and less enthralled by the idea of bearing children and then sitting at home for fifteen years to nurture them before seeking outside interests. Women are making power decisions about money, home or business ownership, and political influence with confidence and ease. As the Indigo energy continues to become more androgynous, these subtle changes will become the norm.

In another few years, Indigos will enter the political realm more actively. Any attempt to hypothesize their political behavior must be just that -- a hypothesis because their future will not be clear for a few more years. However, based on current trends and patterns of behavior, the Indigos will probably carry their openness, honesty, and fairness into the political realm. Today, they are cynical about government and those in government. They are determined not to repeat history. They do not believe in "you scratch my back and I'll scratch yours." They will deal fairly and openly with all groups and all peoples. They exhibit their leadership from within the group, not from an exalted position.

Another welcome change is that the Indigos will enter the world of the media at the same time they enter the political arena. Reporting will be less personal, less slanted, and more fair and honest. They will be more interested in telling the truth than in selling a story with an advertiser's or politician's agenda. They know that any reporting that is less than honest will be spotted and called out within seconds or minutes via social media. A perfect example of this happens today in the fall of corrupt political regimes around the world. The so-called "Twitter Revolutions" in Egypt, Libya, and other countries are the quintessence of Indigo energy. They happened by groups of people coming together for a common cause. They are examples of clear communication and a determination to end corruption. These changes are already happening around the globe. The poorer the country, the more rapid the changes. Indigo children in the poorest developing countries know about and can use cell phones; they understand the concept of being connected to someone they cannot see or might not know.

Nancy Ann Tappe saw the beginning of these changes in a hospital nursery. In the ensuing forty or more years, she has seen the few become many and the many become masses. She has watched their patterns begin to manifest and solidify, studying them intently as she searched for meaning and understanding. Many of her discoveries delighted and intrigued her; some created dismay. All were new, untried, and untested. She has seen young Indigos struggle to assert their personalities at home and at school. She has counseled countless angry youths who have not been able to live up to the Indigo myth that developed around them. But throughout it all, Nancy has focused on the rebirth and renewal that Indigos are bringing to our world through their quiet storm of influence. She continues to see positive energy, positive changes coming about because of their exuberant joy in living, and positive hope for tomorrow.

Other Nancy Tappe Works

Understanding Your Life through Color, 2nd edition by Nancy Ann Tappe.

Back by popular demand! Read what thousands of people have learned about Life Colors, what they mean, and how they affect your life. Understanding Your Life Through Color will provide you with the tools to learn and understand Nancy Tappe, her theory of color, and how it affects the human personality. Available at www.lulu.com.

Understanding Your Life through Awareness. Created by Nancy Tappe and written by Kathy Altaras

This long-awaited compilation of Nancy's lecture and workshop materials provides an overview of her color theory and metaphysical teachings over several decades and explores her lifelong belief in awareness. For those who want to live a more meaningful life, this book is packed with keen insights into human nature and the personality. It is heavily illustrated with charts and diagrams, and it includes the previously published dream book as well as the complete auto / body glossary. Nancy's clientele will find this book easy to read and readily applicable to their own lives. Available at www.lulu.com.

Get the Message: What Your Car Is Trying to Tell You. Created by Nancy Tappe and written by Kathy Altaras.

Start your motors and rev up your engines. Your car is talking to you! *Get the Message* brings you an entirely new perspective on how you view yourself on the highway of life. Have you replaced a battery lately or bought new brakes? Have you been involved in a fender bender? Wasn't your first reaction "why me" or "why now"? *Get the Message* presents an innovative and insightful look at your life and health through the everyday occurrences that your car mirrors back to you. So buckle up your seat belt, sit back, and investigate your own personal warning system that cycles through your car, your dreams, your body, and your life. Available on Amazon.com and your favorite online booksellers.

About Nancy Tappe

Nancy Tappe has often described herself as "an ordinary person with an extraordinary talent." She is, indeed. Nancy's DNA heritage provided her with a combination of synesthesia and "the sight" as her Scottish grandmother might have said. Today scientists define her abilities as accessing and connecting part of the brain that others cannot. Nancy is the owner of Colorology, an organization devoted to the study of the personality through the science of color. Nancy has devoted her life and career to the study of color, consciousness, awareness, and their applications to the human personality. She has a large clientele throughout the United States and in Switzerland. Today Nancy utilizes the magic of technology to disseminate her teachings and philosophy to a world-wide audience through a variety of books and websites. Check her out at www.nancyanntappe.com.

About Kathy Altaras

Kathy Altaras is the owner of Aquila Media Productions, a small, niche-market publishing company specializing in non-fiction media products. She has known and worked with Nancy Tappe for over thirty-five years. A Navy wife of thirty-three years, Kathy had two separate teaching careers in Texas and California, totaling twenty-two years. She holds a lifetime teaching credential in Texas and a California Clear Standard Secondary Teaching Credential. She retired from teaching in California and began consulting for teachers of gifted students. Kathy likes exotic and remote travel, counting Mongolia, Central and South America, and Africa among her favorite places. For more information about her books and other projects, visit www.aquilamediaproductions.com.